THE PURSUIT OF A RUPTURED DUCK

When Kansas Citians went to war...

Edward T. Matheny Jr.

THE PURSUIT OF A RUPTURED DUCK

When Kansas Citians went to war...

By

EDWARD T. MATHENY JR.

A division of Squire Publishers, Inc.
4500 College Blvd.
Leawood, KS 66211
1/888/888-7696

Cover Photo by David Douglas Duncan

Photography Collection, Harry Ransom
Humanities Research Center, The University of Texas at Austin

Copyright 2001
Printed in the United States

ISBN: 1-58597-122-7

Library of Congress Control Number: 2001 0966 74

A division of Squire Publishers, Inc.
4500 College Blvd.
Leawood, KS 66211
1/888/888-7696

A Ruptured Duck

Photo courtesy of Richard D. Blim, M.D.

FOREWORD

FOR THE G.I. GENERATION, memories of World War II will be forever vivid. But well over a half-century has passed, and for new generations that great conflict is history. Increasingly, its contemporaries are a part of history as well — of the 16 million uniformed participants in World War II, more than 1000 die each day.

Arthur Schlesinger, Jr. was in London when World War II ended. For Americans, it had been a long three years, eight months:

> "The war was over. At last.
>
> "Of course, the war was never over for my generation. We pretended it was, went home, picked up the broken threads of our lives. Many sought education under the GI Bill, married the girls they left behind, produced the baby boom and looked always to the future, not the past. The war seemed to slip away, almost as if we were in deliberate denial ..."

Schlesinger noted that "Silence went on for quite a time." Then, later, "one noticed that veterans were beginning to unwrap their memories. Almost for the first time the war generation started telling one another what we had done in the war..." *A Life in the 20th Century,* Arthur M. Schlesinger, Jr., Houghton Mifflin Co., 2000 (Page 352).

* * * * *

According to a Swahili proverb: "Nobody knows where he is going until he knows where he has been."

This memoir is a reminder of where we were, once upon a time.

Admiral Raymond A. Spruance
promised excitement

CINCPAC signs a short snorter

Admiral Charles H. McMorris
His quick yeses and quicker nos
were legendary.

TABLE OF CONTENTS

CHAPTER ONE

Pearl Harbor — A Call To Arms

MOST OF AMERICA'S World War II armed forces were not professional military men but volunteers and draftees who served their country and then, after the battles, returned to civilian life. An honorable discharge entitled veterans to a small lapel pin embossed with an American eagle — we called it a "ruptured duck." Our military careers were spent in pursuit of that duck. In most cases the pin has been mislaid, but not the memories of military service ... it was a part of the times in which we lived.

Today the veterans of World War II, members of a steadily dwindling brotherhood of war, share a common bond of honorable service to our country in history's biggest armed conflict. And somewhere among our memorabilia is our fraternity pin — a ruptured duck.

* * * * *

On December 7, 1941, radio broadcasts made clear the devastation at Pearl Harbor as our Pacific Fleet was reduced to ruin by Japanese bombs. They sank the Arizona and entombed most of her crew, capsized the Oklahoma, left four more battleships dead in the water, and demolished other warships. Nearby air bases were bombed and strafed, their planes destroyed. Almost 3600 men were killed or wounded.

We can all still recall where we were on that Sunday afternoon.

In the quiet college town of Columbia, Missouri, the weekend had begun with a Friday all-school dance featuring Russ Morgan and his big band. We would remember those dance bands, and their music, in the years that lay ahead ... "Nothing, at least for my generation, recalls the past more affectingly than the songs of our youth." (page 137) *A Life in the 20th Century,* supra.

Now, our university world ended as we became part of the G.I. Generation. Those of us in the Sigma Chi fraternity house gathered in the living room, taking comfort in company and staring at our Atwater Kent radio. Conversation was scarce and muted.

The Japanese assault thrust us into World War II; we were spared the divisive debates that would accompany more deliberate entry into later wars. December 7, 1941 — scorned as "a day of infamy" by President Franklin D. Roosevelt — united us and shaped our lives. Pearl Harbor, like the Alamo and the battleship Maine, was something to remember and to avenge. "Remember Pearl Harbor" became a rallying cry. With little dissent, war was declared against Japan on December 8, and against Germany and Italy on December 11.

In the heart of America we didn't know much about the Japanese, half a world away. Newspapers described their pitiless ravaging of China and Southeast Asia. And newsreel films documented in black and white their endless military triumphs. Now, suddenly, we were at war with these savage strangers.

1

Many Americans had perceived expanding Oriental power as "yellow peril" — the attack on Pearl Harbor brought that menace to life. For years white soldiers and politicians had badly underrated the Japanese ability to wage war. And despite what they beheld in the Orient, some scoffed at the new foe — the December 8, 1941 issue of the *Kansas City Journal* editorialized:

> "Japan will soon be out of the picture ... Within a month flimsy Japanese cities will be in ruins and the impoverished islands will be in the stranglehold of a blockade."

But in the same publication Great Britain's pugnacious Prime Minister, Sir Winston Churchill, cautioned against "any tendency to underestimate Japan's military and naval strength."

*****

In Kansas City, recruiting offices were immediately swamped — in the first few hours of December 8, there were 25 applicants for Marine enlistments and over 200 Navy applications. Many were youths of seventeen and eighteen, well below the draft age of twenty-one.

Dr. Maxwell Berry, married with two small children, was practicing medicine in Kansas City on December 7:

> "Josephine and I sat up long after our 2 kids were in bed that night. We agreed that I had no other choice than to do whatever I could to defend our children and our family." *One Man's WW II,* Maxwell Berry, 1998, p.12.

On December 8, 1941, Max volunteered for military service.

One of the Navy applicants was Clifford C. Jones Jr., who was sworn in as a deck officer candidate on December 17, 1941. Cliff's father was out of the city at the time and missed the ceremony, but arranged an encore which he witnessed. In April, 1942, the twice-sworn Cliff reported for midshipman school at Northwestern University's Abbott Hall in downtown Chicago.

Hayne Ellis, a retired rear admiral, volunteered to head Kansas City's Department of Civilian Defense — one of the war's many "dollar a year" men. Ellis' department would quickly outgrow its small office on the twenty-fourth floor of City Hall, enlisting volunteers for everything from sewing and knitting to psychiatrist and rhythm band director. (Before the end of the war, eighty-four-year-old Lillian Magness would devote 24,000 hours to sewing bandages and 700 hours to knitting.)

*****

In Columbia, reactions on the University of Missouri campus were varied. In my history class, those who were disposed to "eat, drink and be merry for tomorrow we die" were rebuked by Professor John B. Wolf: "That's all well and good if you die, but what if you live — and most of you will ?" A few volunteered for the armed forces, but President Roosevelt declared that college students could best serve their country by remaining in school until called to active duty. So, most of us awaited "Greetings" from the draft board or sought to avoid buck private status by applying to officer candidate schools.

The deadliness of war was out of sight. There were no television screens in America's living rooms to disclose the carnage of the battlefield.

Pearl Harbor's bombs sounded the death knell of an innocent age at the University. Post-war college life would be quite different — returning veterans, matured by wartime experiences and financed by the G.I. Bill, would crowd the classrooms; "temporary" buildings would disfigure the campus for decades; and some colorful traditions would be lost, as well as sophomoric high jinks. But for now, in the brief twilight of an era, students affectionately clung to familiar campus activities and customs. In the words of Britain's Winston Churchill: "The old world at its sunset was fair to see."

Mizzou's "BMOCs" (Big Men On Campus) sported key chains decorated with the insignia of various honorary and scholastic organizations. Patrons of scruffy, popular Jack's Shack carved their initials in the beer-soaked wooden tables, and ten-cent coke dates — often "Dutch treat" — at Gaebler's Black and Gold Inn featured dancing on the mezzanine for couples who could afford to feed the nickelodeon. Charlie Spivak played "the sweetest trumpet this side of heaven" at the Pan-Hel Ball where the decorations were red, white and blue. Those caught walking on the lawn of the College of Agriculture ran the gauntlet of an Ag School paddle line. And the matched pair of Chinese stone lions guarding the School of Journalism reputedly roared whenever a virgin passed between them.

* * * * *

I had made the M.U. basketball team as a sophomore, and looked forward to a scheduled trip to the West Coast. When war was declared, that trip hung in the balance and my outrage over Pearl Harbor was tempered by the survival of our travel plans. Unlike today's collegians we traveled by rail, my taller teammates uncomfortably telescoped into Pullman berths at night. Among them was another sophomore, my future brother-in-law, Earl R. Stark.

At this early stage, the war was far removed from the college towns we visited on our journey. In Moscow, Idaho and Spokane, Washington, we turned to the sports section before we read the front page of the local newspapers.

Apprehension was fostered on the West Coast by rumors of Japanese submarines lying in ambush off the California shore. The submarine rumors were not farfetched. Soon German U-boats were attacking shipping off the Atlantic Coast — during one nine-day stretch in May, 1942, three ships were torpedoed off Florida.

Following our return to Columbia, we gathered around a small radio in the locker room at Brewer Fieldhouse to root for Mizzou's football team in their 1942 New Year's Day Sugar Bowl game against the Rams of Fordham University. We learned later that the game was played in a sea of mud and rain, but zealous wartime censors forbade any radio reference to the New Orleans weather. The final score, 2 - 0 in favor of Fordham, reflected the sloppy conditions.

* * * * *

Herman Johnson, already a college graduate with a master's degree, was working at the War Production Board in Washington, D.C. when President Roosevelt declared that all able-bodied men should be in uniform. Herman responded — he joined the Army and in January 1942 was dispatched to the Tuskeegee Army Air Field in Tuskeegee, Alabama as a personnel officer.

This was the birthplace of a remarkable group of World War II pilots, the Tuskeegee Airmen. They were the first African-Americans to qualify as military pilots in any branch of the armed forces. Young African-Americans came from everywhere to Tuskeegee to learn to fly, and the first group received their wings on March 7, 1942. For every pilot, there was ground support needed including mechanics and Herman Johnson formed training schools for that purpose, recruiting in Alabama and Mississippi. The original flying instructors were white, but no bias or prejudice was evident during instruction. "The personnel at Tuskeegee were integrated, with no racial problems." Herman Johnson.

* * * * *

Dr. Maxwell Berry was inducted as a Captain, Medical Corps, A.U.S., at Ft. Douglas, Utah on May 10, 1942.

* * * * *

In the ensuing months, the war's impact on the University was relentless.

Familiar faces quietly disappeared ... one day they were there, the next day they were gone, as the nation's military needs took their inexorable toll on the student body.

Tire shortages limited student travel, and an Associated Press item on May 19, 1942, reported:

"The tire exigency caused cancellation of a trip by 300 University of Missouri coeds to attend a dance at Fort Leonard Wood last month.

"The soldiers didn't take the disappointment lightly. They sent a petition to the War Department and Saturday night 300 of them will call on the coeds in 20 Army trucks."

The introduction to the University's 1942 yearbook noted the changes:

"Here it is — your SAVITAR, built of the days when a radio program meant Fred Waring or Glenn Miller, and a blackout was something they had in Europe and copied at the I.M/A. dance; and some of the days after a Sunday morning in early December when Pearl Harbor became more than a name on a map to us. It cannot help but be a memorable book — it has been a memorable year. We give it to you with a great sigh of relief, but with a feeling that it is more than a yearbook — it is a milestone."

* * * * *

The University of Missouri was a land grant college, and the Morrill Act of 1862 made military training in the University's R.O.T.C. field artillery unit compulsory for freshman and sophomore men. However, few of us had taken the program seriously. Even the horses that pulled the field artillery batteries were not totally committed to the military — they moonlighted as mounts for the University's polo team. To escape the boredom of the weekly parades, three of us alternated in attendance — wearing heavy, one-size-fits-all uniforms, we took turns answering roll call from the anonymous rear rank. But now, confronted with World War II, we found the gold collar bars, tailored uniform and status of a second lieutenant attractive, and the military science courses benefitted accordingly.

CHAPTER TWO

The Early Warriors of '42

COLLEGE GRADUATES in the spring of 1942 soon found themselves members of the armed forces. Among them was Kansas Citian Clinton W. Kanaga Jr., who joined the Marines in May 1942. Following OCS at Quantico, Virginia, Lieutenant Kanaga boarded the ocean liner Matsonia for a two-week trip to New Zealand and the war in the South Pacific.

James M. Kemper Jr. received his draft notice before completion of his senior year at Yale. An accomplished horseman, he was inducted as a horse cavalry volunteer in July 1942 and sent to Officers Candidate School at Fort Riley, Kansas. "That branch of the service was full of horse athletes like jockeys, horse trainers, polo players, cowboys and Western ranch types." James M. Kemper Jr.

Frank M. Cortelyou Jr. was commissioned a Navy ensign on July 13, 1942. An M.U. engineering school graduate, Frank joined Company B, 20th Battalion, of the Navy's Construction Battalions (CBs or Seabees) — the Seabees, comprised largely of experienced construction workers, had been formally organized just four months earlier. Frank sailed for New Caledonia in the South Pacific on October 6, 1942; he succinctly noted the departure: "Out under the Gate Bridge — and last look at the U.S." *Personal Log*. Ens. F. M. Cortelyou Jr.

Cliff Jones graduated from midshipman school and requested destroyer duty, but was ordered to remain at Northwestern as an instructor in seamanship even though he had never been to sea. After nine months as an instructor, Cliff's wish was granted — he was assigned to the USS Luce, DD 522, a new destroyer.

Herman Johnson took the Tuskeegee Air Force Band on a war bond tour. The jazz music of the big band was a great success, and a Treasury Department citation recognized the outstanding sales results.

Robert Con Hanger, who had enlisted in the Marines before graduation, reported for OCS Boot Camp, also in Quantico, in November 1942.

F.L. (Tom) Thompson enlisted in the Army Air Corps in December 1942.

William H. Woodson and his older brother Winston Allen Woodson were commissioned Navy ensigns on Christmas Eve 1942, following graduation from midshipman school at Northwestern University. Bill Woodson was assigned to the battleship Colorado, the only battleship of the Pacific Fleet to avoid the Pearl Harbor holocaust ... by chance, the Colorado was undergoing overhaul at the Bremerton, Washington Navy Yard on December 7, 1941. Allen was assigned to the heavy cruiser New Orleans.

* * * * *

George Washingon Tourtellot III received his draft notice in October 1941. He had just turned twenty-seven and the maximum age for selective service was twenty-eight. At Kansas City's Union Station, Private Tourtellot boarded a troop train for Fort Leavenworth. He anticipated less than a year's service, but two months later came Pearl Harbor and George was in "for the duration."

George owned a photography business ... Miracle Pictures, Inc.: "If it's good it's a Miracle." He applied for Officer Candidate School with attachment to the Signal Corps. He was accepted and in March 1942 he began three months' officer's training at Ft. Monmouth, New Jersey.

George applied for the Signal Corps because it was the photographic unit of the U.S. Army. However, the Signal Corps also had established a radar research unit at Fort Monmouth.

On June 3, George Tourtellot emerged from OCS a second lieutenant, a "ninety-day wonder." And on June 6, George married Sally Kaney at her home in Kansas City, Missouri.

A Ft. Monmouth test disclosed that George Tourtellot — a graduate engineer from the University of Michigan — had an exceptional IQ, and he was sent to Harvard to work on a highly secret research project. The project was radar.

Because of the importance of radar, measures for jamming and anti-jamming were developed. In March 1942, the Radio Research Lab was established at Harvard, and designed various anti-jamming devices which the Signal Corps added to Army radar.

On June 15, Lieutenant Tourtellot began his tour of duty at Harvard with a two-week training course in the graduate school of engineering, where the subject was alternating currents. Then, on July 1, George began another course under the same auspices. The subject was "Electronics and Cathode Ray Tubes." This was new territory for many people ... about this time, George received a letter from a Navy physician that ended: "P.S. What is (are) electronics anyway?" The course required George's constant exposure to cathode ray tubes until it was completed on September 22.

Another secret radar project was established at Massachusetts Institute of Technology (MIT) ... the Radiation Laboratory, or Rad Lab. Here were developed microwave radars, which were more resistant to jamming.

On October 1, George began a special full-time course at MIT, where he was constantly exposed to ultrahigh frequency techniques. The MIT course was completed on December 31, 1942.

Although he did not know it at the time, George Tourtellot was already a war casualty:

"What he was doing was highly secret. He was researching radar. It has been written of the Second World War that while the atom bomb ended the war, radar won the war.

"George and I didn't know until the early 1960s that the project he worked on would cost him his life. That was the final diagnosis — it was the exposure to ultrahigh frequency and cathode rays that caused the strange illness that took him before he reached the age of 50 years." *The War Years*, the Journal of Sally Kaney Tourtellot Ruddy.

From MIT, George was sent to the Southern Signal Corps School, Camp Murphy, Florida, for further radar training. That training, completed April 8, 1943, qualified George as a radar officer, a radar officer technical, and an air warning officer — with a technical rating of "excellent."

CHAPTER THREE

College Life Diminished

MOVIES DEPICTING American heroism and enemy atrocities stimulated patriotic fervor; after one particularly effective film, fearful that the conflict would end before I could participate, I attempted to enlist in the Marine Corps' officer candidate school only to discover that near-sighted astigmatism disqualified me for OCS. The Selective Service Board would not be that selective when I registered for the draft, and my interest in the Tiger Battery of the field artillery was heightened even further. Then, on September 15, 1942, I was accepted as an apprentice seaman in the Navy's V 7 program for deck officer candidates. (Forewarned, I solved the astigmatism problem by sneaking an advance peek at the eye chart in the Kansas City Navy recruiting office.)

V 7 meant continuation of my college education as a civilian. I returned to the Columbia campus in the autumn of 1942 for my junior year. A history major, I had dodged mathematics courses, but now at the Navy's insistence I added trigonometry to my academic curriculum. I was relieved to discover that the Navy's requirement would be satisfied if I audited the trig course, sparing my grade point average from disaster.

* * * * *

I had been sports editor of the *1942 Savitar*. The senior slated to manage the yearbook's 1943 edition had entered the armed forces, and I found myself the new editor-in-chief.

Mizzou's former All American quarterback, "Pitchin' Paul" Christman, also returned to the campus — not as a football hero, but as a chief petty officer attached to a naval training school offering instruction in the operation and maintenance of diesel engines. Seamen enrolled in the training school were entertained at dances sponsored by patriotic young ladies from Columbia's Stephens and Christian colleges.

In 1942, Stephens College began to train women as aviators for the commercial air transportation industry — the first American college to do so — and ten percent of the women aviators who served during World War II received their initial training in Columbia.

The ASTP (Army Specialized Training Program) commandeered the Sigma Chi house, and we regrouped in a rooming house behind The Huddle, a campus pool hall. Our energetic landlady, a large Irish woman named Hazel O'Shaugnessy, stoked her coal furnace, shoveled snow from sidewalks, and enforced some measure of decorum within our dwindling ranks.

Attrition among the student body persisted. Operating year-round, on an accelerated wartime schedule, Mizzou could graduate a student in two years eight months. However, the education of most young men was interrupted by military service.

An organization called the "Student War Board" fostered physical fitness, entertainment of servicemen, war bond sales and other supportive activities, and sponsored a scrap metal drive that culminated in the Junk Dealer's Ball.

Although normal University social life was drastically curtailed, intercollegiate sports were encouraged as a boost to the nation's morale. Wartime tunes dominated radio's Lucky Strike Hit Parade — the Andrews Sisters' rendition of "The Boogie Woogie Bugle Boy of Company B" was a particular favorite. However, fraternity and sorority parties were neither as frequent nor as lavish as in prior years, and there were few all school dances; exceptions were the Wednesday night Jesse Jumps held in venerable Jesse Hall, the proceeds of which went to activities supporting the armed forces.

The M.U. campus was representative of the country's universities in one respect — there were no anti-war protests.

* * * * *

The *Kansas City Journal* retreated from its December 8, 1941 posture that predicted an early end to the war. The *Journal's* March 2, 1942 edition described imaginary Japanese raids on Kansas City — fiction like Orson Welles' famous Martian invasion hoax. Headlined "This Might Be Any Day In 1942," the lead story began:

"Three waves of Japanese bombers ripped apart the Heart of America today. The Rising Sun pilots wrote in the shambles of Kansas City a story even more ghastly than did the Nazis at England's Coventry. Thousands died in their homes, hospitals and on the streets."

Another story, a fictitious interview with Admiral Hayne Ellis, quoted the Civilian Defense director: "Every man must do his duty now. Police are instructed to shoot on sight every looter. Any person who refuses to obey the orders of uniformed policemen and firemen may be treated as deserters in battle deserve. This is battle."

The paper's most imaginative account described remorseful suicides:

"Twelve men whose bodies were found beside an undemolished portion of the Art Gallery were said by police not to have been victims of the enemy. All of them, F.B.I. agents said, had ended their own lives when they realized their mistake in believing 'it couldn't happen here.'"

Each *Journal* story ended with "It could happen here any day."

CHAPTER FOUR

The War is Real for Some

CLINT KANAGA'S WAR was very real in the South Pacific ... the battle for strategic Guadalcanal in the Solomon Islands. It was the first American ground offensive of World War II. Before organized Japanese resistance ended on February 9, 1943, Clint distinguished himself as leader of a machine gun platoon in the 'Canal's jungle fighting — a performance that led his company commander, Kansas Citian William K. Jones (later a general commanding the Fleet Marine Force, Pacific) to recommend him for the Navy Cross. "On Guadalcanal I started out with a machine gun platoon of forty-five and ended up six and a half weeks later with twenty-two." Clint Kanaga.

The Seabees' first appearance in a combat zone was also on Guadacanal, constructing military works in a remarkably short time. On New Caledonia, where the 20th Battalion was engaged in construction and stevedoring, Frank Cortelyou wrote in his *Log*: "February 10, 1943 Heard reports that Guadalcanal was all ours." Three weeks later there was another report — a cable informed Frank that he was a father: "Girl. Both Fine, Love. Betty Cortelyou."

Henry W. Bloch, who with his younger brother Richard would later found H & R Block, applied for the aviation cadet program while at the University of Michigan, and was called to active duty in early 1943. He was dispatched to Texas for training.

Also in early 1943, Albert C. Bean Jr. used some extra credit hours to graduate early from Cornell University and reported to midshipman school at Columbia University. The midshipman graduates were given their choice of ship and ocean, for service. Ace chose destroyer duty in the Pacific and a close friend chose destroyer duty in the Atlantic. The assignments were reversed; Ace was ordered to report to the USS MacKenzie, serving in the Atlantic, and the friend was sent to a Pacific destroyer. Within six months, the friend in the Pacific was killed. Ace boarded the MacKenzie in the Brooklyn Navy Yard and went through the war unscathed.

On February 17, 1943, a talented young photographer, David Douglas Duncan, enlisted in the U.S. Marine Corps. He informed his parents in Kansas City: "Childhood and youth are finished. Only He knows how much of my race has been run. Today I have been accepted by the United Stated Marine Corps." *Yankee Nomad*, David Douglas Duncan, 1966, p.11. Duncan completed his basic training at Quantico and then became a combat photographer in the Pacific Theater as a Marine lieutenant.

About this same time, Bill Woodson caught up with his ship, the Colorado, in the Fiji Islands. He made the long trip from San Francisco aboard a troop ship.

Kansas City's Department of Civilian Defense had two mounted police troops: Troop A, a group of thirty-six riders from the Ararat Shrine Mounted Guard, and Troop B, whose forty-four khaki-clad "stockyard rangers" headed by Captain Frederic H. Olander Sr. provided armed guards for the stockyards. Mr. Olander had been a field artillery captain in the first World War.

Captain Olander's son, Fred Jr., on February 19, 1943, boarded a streetcar to report for aviation cadet training. His first government check, for ten cents, reimbursed him for car fare to the Army Air Corps office in Kansas City, Kansas.

Redman Callaway, newly commissioned a second lieutenant in the Army's Quartermaster Corps, in February 1943 took command of an African-American truck company. Red had joined the Army in April, 1941 ... faced with a one-year hitch as a prewar draftee, he had elected to confront the inevitable ahead of schedule (a "handcuff volunteer" in the vernacular of the day) but the December 1941 assault on Pearl Harbor changed Red's timetable.

Redman Callaway's hometown, Kansas City, Missouri, was almost totally segregated in 1943, and his contact with African-Americans was minimal. As he later wrote: "Nothing in my experience had prepared me for this command." Red's adventures are recounted in his absorbing, informative *White Captain *** Black Troops*, The Lowell Press, Inc., Kansas City, Missouri, 1993.

William N. Deramus, an assistant trainmaster with the Wabash Railroad, was called to active duty with the Army the end of April. He and other Wabash officials reported to the Officer Training Corps of the Transportation Corps for a six-week course in basic military training and transportation. They graduated in June, and their unit was activated June 25, 1943, in New Orleans, Louisiana.

Jim Kemper, now a second lieutenant, was assigned to the 24th Cavalry Regiment in Laredo, Texas, a Texas National Guard Regiment. (Jim's brother, David Woods Kemper, was assigned to the 2nd Cavalry Division in Bracketville, Texas — in a horse cavalry regiment of African-Americans under white officers.) Jim's tour of duty with the 24th was brief:

> "When I first reported for drill, the stable sergeant asked me if I had ridden very much, and I told him I had a little. So he had a docile mare led out, and I climbed aboard. As I moved down the column of troopers lined up in front of the colonel, I lifted my leg to check the girth and all hell broke loose. The mare pitched me over her head right in front of the colonel. A few days later, orders arrived for my transfer to Headquarters Troop of the 56th Cavalry Brigade which was the commanding brigade for our regiment. Although at the time it seemed unjust, it turned out that I traveled in much better style mechanized than I would have on a horse and eventually wound up with heavy weapons, heavy machine guns and a 37-millimeter cannon as well as reconnaissance assignments overseas. For anyone who loved horses, being in the horse cavalry was a great experience, but it was no way to fight a modern war." James M. Kemper Jr.

Gordon H. Robertson entered the Navy aviation cadet program in July 1942 as a member of the first class at Olathe Naval Air Station, Olathe, Kansas. By May of 1943, he had qualified in carrier landings and that June he joined Bombing Squadron Two ... a dive bombing squadron, whose two-man crews consisted of pilot and rear seat gunner-radioman. Only two aviators in the squadron had combat experience but theirs was impressive — they participated in the decisive Battle of Midway.

More advanced training "provided many interesting moments for the relatively inexperienced naval aviators" according to Gordon. Night flying in formation was a particular challenge, requiring an orderly landing sequence with adequate intervals between aircraft. One of these drills ended with Gordon and his plane in Rhode Island's Narragansett Bay:

> "After I landed, the air traffic controller in the tower said, in a rather excited voice, 'plane on the runway, keep it rolling!' This instruction was repeated. I had visions of a squadron mate, having landed long, about to chew up my tail. Unable to see directly ahead, I kept power on to maintain speed after landing. Shortly after seeing some red lights (runway end

lights) pass below my wing, I felt a couple of bumps and then felt water rising around me. I had sailed into Narraganset Bay, past the end of the runway. A short swim back to the sea-wall, and with the aid of the crash crew I was soon back on dry land no worse for the error. Squadron mates from time to time afterward referred to me as 'Duck.'" Gordon Robertson.

Another Kansas Citian, Navy V 7 deck officer candidate John R. Wells, graduated from the University of Kansas that spring and was immediately ordered to report to midshipman school at the University of Notre Dame.

David W. Robinson, M.D., completed a general surgery residency at the University of Kansas Medical School and enlisted in the Medical Corps of the Army in June, 1943. He was commissioned a first lieutenant and reported for duty at Fort Dix, New Jersey. There ensued further training in neurosurgery and plastic surgery at Columbia Presbyterian Hospital in New York City, and then an intensive six-week course in the treatment of burns at the Army's best facility for this specialty, Valley Forge Hospital near Philadelphia, Pennsylvania.

Jack B. O'Hara, a talented artist pursuing a Chicago advertising career, volunteered for the armed service but was rejected by both the Marine Corps and the Navy because of bad eyesight. He was accepted as an Army draftee, however, for "limited service." Following ninety days' basic infantry training at Camp Roberts, California, Jack's platoon went into combat on a Pacific island … but without Jack, who was sent to the Medical Administrative Corps' Officer Candidate School at Camp Barkley, Texas.

At OCS, the officer candidates marched to and from class, swinging their arms in cadence. When a drill instructor extended his hand to correct O'Hara's arm swing, Jack mistakenly shook it, gaining him special recognition at his graduation ceremony.

Jack O'Hara emerged from OCS a second lieutenant and in due course was assigned to the Kansas City Medical Depot. His duties there included receipt of medical supplies, the subject of a cartoon that he sketched for the front page of the *Depot Journal*.

* * * * *

The second week in July, 1943, George Tourtellot boarded a troop train for a port of embarcation near Seattle, Washington. He was destined for the Aleutian Islands, where with a platoon of men he would set up radar stations at various island locations. George would not see Sally again for two years, nine months.

Life in the frozen North was not without humor — George wrote of visiting a bar whose decor featured a brassiere of very generous proportions with the admonition "Remember Pearl Hogan."

* * * * *

Frank Cortelyou's Seabees left New Caledonia and on July 26 came ashore on Woodlark Island in the Solomon Sea. Upon learning of the pending move, Frank wrote in his *Log*: "Think this will be a big boost to the morale of men as they were figuring we were sidetracked and stuck here for the duration 'cause we were unfit for front line duty."

In addition to rifle, gas mask and helmet, Frank carried jungle gear including machette, green face paint, and camouflage suit. The 20th's landing on Woodlark was unopposed, but there would be frequent bombing raids.

* * * * *

The latter part of July, Max Berry left California for Australia on a converted Dutch ocean liner as

Chief of Medical Services for the 117th Station Hospital. His ship docked in Brisbane on August 13, 1943, and on August 29 the unit started north through the Coral Sea for Port Moresby, New Guinea to establish a hospital. When they disembarked in New Guinea, Hospital personnel were greeted by a huge Aussie banner proclaiming: "Through these portals passes the best damned mosquito bait in the world." *One Man's WW II*, supra, p.6.

The hospital was still under construction on October 3 when Max wrote his "Dearest Josephine:"

"We worked until noon building and then took Sunday afternoon off to get dressed up in field outfits, helmets, pistols, belts and leggings to be presented with a campaign ribbon. I don't know what the hell I'm going to do with a campaign ribbon." *One Man's WW II*, supra, p.89.

* * * * *

After sinking a German U-boat and destroying German tanks and guns ashore while supporting General George Patton's invasion of Sicily, on October 18, 1943 the MacKenzie suffered her only significant damage ... but not in battle. The events of that day are described in the ship's official history:

"On 18 October 1943 after fueling at Queen's Dock, Swansea, England, (the MacKenzie) was ordered to shift berths, with the assistance of two tugs. While passing Scherzer Bridge the bow tug's tow line parted and the MacKenzie's starboard anchor scraped one of the supports of the operating rack on the bridge. As she entered King's Dock she was swung clockwise in order that the bow would pass through the swing bridge first. The ship's engines were used to assist in swinging the bow east, but resulted in the stern swinging to port, parting the stern tug's tow line, and backing the MacKenzie into a sand sucker. Upon resuming forward motion she hit the north wall of the Prince of Wales Dock, and while backing down, lightly, hit a tug boat before sternway could be checked. Resuming forward motion the starboard anchor was dropped, but before headway could be checked she hit the minesweeper HMS Fairfax. On clearing the Fairfax the anchor was heaved in, and the Mackenzzie prepared to head for her berth. However, the swinging stern lightly hit another minesweeper, and the anchor was again dropped and all way checked. The commanding officer then ordered the ship secured in any berth which appeared available. A line was passed to the north seawall and secured to a bollard astern of the Fairfax. After running over one of the buoys located in the middle of the dock, the ship was warped into a berth on the north side of the Prince of Wales Dock. Damages resulting from this series of collisions necessitated a forty-one day delay for repairs." Division of Naval History, Ships' Histories Section, Navy Department.

The MacKenzie's skipper later made admiral.

* * * * *

The first of the Tuskeegee Airmen to go overseas, the 99th Squadron, deployed to North Africa in May, 1943. The following November, Herman Johnson joined another Tuskeegee squadron, the 101st, in North Africa as their disbursing officer. The Airmen initially flew P-40 Warhawks over North Africa, Sicily and Italy.

* * * * *

On November 13, Max Berry's new hospital in New Guinea began taking patients, most of them flown in from combat zones 100 or more miles away. The hospital would operate above capacity until it closed ten months later when the medical unit followed the war north.

The following day, General Douglas MacArthur inspected the 117th:

"We had been warned he was hipped on latrines so we dug a deep new 10-holer for the dysentary ward; double-screened and loaded with lime.

"The inspection team came in a long train of vehicles, mostly jeeps, with high ranking officers. There was a swarm of reporters. (Lieutenant Albert) Johnson was chosen as the guide.

"MacArthur was a ramrod straight, handsome officer, totally pleasant but serious ... He said to Johnson, 'Lieutenant, show me the latrine.' He saw the double-screened double doors, looked down one hole, and said 'How deep is this?' to which Johnson replied, 'Ten feet, suh.' There was no further conversation. After several photographs with Lt. Colonel Arn, he got stiffly into the jeep and the convoy took off in a cloud of dust." *One Man's WW II*, supra, p.43.

* * * * *

Bob Hanger, now a twenty-two-year old Marine second lieutenant, landed on a small island in the South Pacific the latter part of November ... it was part of the bloody Tarawa operation that would claim 1027 Marine lives and 2292 wounded in just four days (the Japanese would lose practically their entire complement of defenders, 4690.)

Two days after the Marines waded ashore on Tarawa, Cliff Jones' Luce set sail from Pearl Harbor to join a task force in the Aleutian Islands. There it engaged in diversionary attacks on the Kurile Islands, the war's first land bombardment of the Japanese homeland.

Ensign Gordon Robertson's squadron, provided with new model dive bombers, the SB2C Curtis Helldiver, embarked for the Pacific Theater aboard a new aircraft carrier, the USS Hornet (CV 12). This ship replaced an earlier Hornet (CV 8) ... the carrier that as "Shangri La" had launched the historic Doolittle bombing raid on Tokyo in April 1942 had been sunk by the Japanese on August 26, 1942, in the Battle of the Santa Cruz Islands.

Clint Kanaga contracted malaria on Guadalcanal and lost fifty-five pounds. Following treatment in New Zealand and San Diego, he returned to Kansas City on sick leave. After regaining his health, he was assigned to the USS Elmore, an attack transport, for further duty in the Pacific Theater.

Cornelius E. Lombardi Sr., a prominent Kansas City attorney, was awarded the silver star for gallantry in action in the first World War. His son, Cornelius E. Lombardi Jr., dropped out of Yale after his freshman year to enlist in the Marine Corps. Following boot camp in San Diego, Private Lombardi was assigned sea duty. As he wrote in the war memoir prepared for his family, *Some Reminiscences of World War II*, February 2002:

"Every large navy ship from cruiser on up has a Marine detachment. Their assignment is basically guard duty — and theoretically to be ready for an emergency landing, although this is a very remote possibility. In reality, they serve as captain's orderlies and guard the brig, and their battle station is on anti-aircraft guns. They are considered (at least by themselves) an elite group. The infantrymen have a different idea, referring to them as 'seagoing bellhops.' " page 11.

While in sea school, Neil was told by an instructor that the light cruiser St.Louis was " a jinxed ship that had had a terrible run of bad luck." He was assigned to the St.Louis.

In December 1943, Grant B. Hatfield, D.D.S., two months out of dental school, reported for duty at Carlisle Barracks, Pennsylvania. There was no dentistry ... "We drilled every day on our feet — not in the mouth." Grant Hatfield.

George Berry, many years later the distinguished Judge of the Probate Court of Jackson County but in October 1943 a second lieutenant in the Army field artillery, had his closest call of the war on the firing range at Camp Adair, in Corvallis, Oregon. His driver took a late afternoon shortcut through the target area, in the mistaken belief that gunnery practice had ceased for the day. When an artillery round exploded close by, Lieutenant Berry protected himself by rolling up the vehicle's windows.

Also in December, Bill Deramus — now the Trainmaster of an Army Transportation Company with the rank of captain — embarked for India, setting sail on his birthday.

CHAPTER FIVE

The Home Front Goes to War

AWARE THAT MY COLLEGE DAYS could be interrupted at any time, I had entered Missouri University's 1943 summer school program, hoping to graduate before being called to active duty. Classrooms were not air conditioned, and Dr. Elmer Ellis' musty medieval history class was soporific on those drowsy summer mornings — especially if there had been a poker game the night before. But I was rewarded for my industry. When V 7 participants were ordered to report to organized, uniformed V 12 units, the order excepted "certain individuals who had one term or less in college to complete for their baccalaureate degree." And the M.U. faculty approved my accelerated graduation "without meeting minor requirements."

I graduated unceremoniously on December 23, 1943.

Marking time at home, I grew increasingly uncomfortable with civilian status. By this time, 40,000 Kansas Citians and 450,000 Missourians were off to war. Enrollment at M.U. had plummeted below 2000 in 1943. Most of my friends were in uniform, military service disclosed by blue stars in the windows of their homes and on pins worn by their mothers. My straight-arrow generation had been innoculated by parents, teachers and scoutmasters with patriotism and loyalty, values sustaining them on distant battlefields. All were patriots. The war would be the biggest event in our lifetime. Virtually every able-bodied young man would participate and I wanted to be a part of it.

* * * * *

World War II was all-consuming on the home front. Although Kansas City was far from the theaters of war, there were 7500 air raid wardens — one for each block. Guards protected the city's public utilities and strict security was in place at factories engaged in defense production. "Rosie the Riveter" and "Wanda the Welder" labored in Kansas City's Pratt & Whitney aircraft engine plant, and for 63 cents an hour built B-25 "Billy Mitchell" medium bombers at the North American Aviation plant where half the employees were women. General Doolittle's raiders flew B-25s.

Two-thirds of all of the B-25s produced during World War II came from Kansas City, and in 1944 the city became the sole producer of B-25s for all theaters of the war. The plant operated twenty-four hours a day, and future Congressman Larry Winn, a stellar high school athlete before he lost a leg in a teen-age boating accident, supervised a 'round-the-clock recreation program for employees — dances, softball, baseball, and tennis. He also served as sports editor and columnist for the plant newspaper, "The North Amera-Kansan."

In *Ordinary People, Extraordinary Lives*, a collection of interviews by students of Shawnee Mission East High School in Johnson County, Kansas, there is this exchange:

"While the men were at war, what did the women do on the home front?"

"Well, we had to do a lot of the men's work. I built B-25 bombers, the ones with the devil tail thing — they're big bombers, and they were the first ones to bomb Tokyo. I was the inspector. I was happy that I could do something for the war effort, but it was kind of sad to think that it would go and bomb people. But when I was the inspector, the rivets ... when they weren't just right, why, I'd make them drill them out again and put in good ones. And I said: 'Well, if you were to ride in it, you'd want a good rivet in there.' I felt like I was doing my part. It was my way to serve the country ..." Emma Lou, an inspector. Born 1921 (Page 96).

* * * * *

Thousands of LCTs (landing craft tanks) and LCMs (landing craft mechanized) were constructed by the Darby Products of Steel Company and the Kansas City Structural Steel Company, of Kansas City, Kansas. The Sunflower Munitions Plant in Kansas and the Lake City Arsenal in Missouri produced ammunition. Glider assemblage, for invasion use, replaced livestock expositions in Kansas City's American Royal building ... a facility second only to the Ford Motor Company in the number of gliders produced. And Butler Manufacturing Company landing mats went to Omaha Beach for D Day.

Quotas for blood donations and war bond sales were regularly exceeded. "Everything was goal-driven." Larry Winn. (*Over Here, The Story of Kansas City and World War II*, KCPT 19.) Winn assisted in the recruiting of blood donors for the American Red Cross.

Civilian Defense volunteers signed on as auxiliary policemen, firemen, blood donors, nurses and ambulance drivers, and collected salvage metal, rubber and grease. Kansas City led the nation in the number of pounds of grease collected per capita; young "salvage commandos" from Gladstone Elementary School marched from house to house, stopping at every corner to sing "Praise the Lord and Pass the Ammunition." High school boys were trained to send Morse Code messages by flashlight, practicing transmissions from the rooftop of The Walnuts apartments at 5049 Wornall Road. *A City at War: The Impact of the Second World War on Kansas City*, by Frederick Marcel Spletstoser, Kansas City, Missouri 1971 (Western Missouri Historical Manuscript Collection at University of Missouri-Kansas City).

Kansas City's high schools joined forces to buy a bomber through the sale of defense stamps ... the price for one bomber: $175,000. And at the city's Southwest High School, students made ash trays out of tin cans for the U.S.O. They also helped distribute ration books but reported difficulty in persuading women to disclose their ages as required by law.

Newsreel pictures of Adolph Hitler were booed by movie-goers. And when a woman in a Kansas City bakery expressed the hope that the war would last so she could pay off her mortgage "somebody slammed a lemon pie in her face." Page 23, *LIFE Celebrates 1945*, Special Collections Edition, June 5, 1995.

The farmers of Missouri became "soldiers of the soil," supplemented by urban "victory gardens." Coupons, ration books, points and tokens regulated everything from the purchase of gasoline (four gallons per week for personal use) to consumption of sugar. Military applications were found for items formerly thrown away — waste fats and old silk stockings were used to manufacture munitions, and floss from milkweed pods buoyed airmens' "Mae West" life jackets named for the buxom movie star.

Another exchange from *Ordinary People, Extraordinary Lives*, supra, was this interview:

"What experience has left a memorable impression on your life?"

"World War II. Definitely World War II ... My father was gone for quite a long time because he was in the Navy. That probably is what I remember the most. I don't remember much of anything that happened before that, but I can remember that long, lengthy time that he wasn't home ... And I remember there were certain things that you couldn't get at the grocery store ... they had a lot of rationing ... because they were in short supply. I remember my mother had a garden because you had to have food to eat, and so everybody was planting gardens and canning vegetables and fruits — that kind of thing. Those really were my earliest memories, but as you get older, you realize that that particular war really was the basis for a lot of things that happened … World War II changed everything." Sherrel, a woman. Born 1941. (Page 116)

CHAPTER SIX

Ninety-Day Wonder

FOLLOWING MY GRADUATION, two months expired without a call to arms. But finally, there arrived a slim envelope bearing the return address of the Ninth Naval District. My orders to midshipman school at last.

Detroit's assembly lines were celebrated for mass production. World War II midshipman schools were equally efficient. I had seen the ocean for the first time during our basketball trip to the West Coast. I had never set foot on the deck of a ship. Now I would be a naval officer after just three months' training.

A single sheet of paper summoned me to U.S. Naval Training School, Plattsburg Barracks, Plattsburg, New York ... to report on March 6th, 1944, and "not before." I was to bring with me toilet articles, bedroom slippers (no wooden clogs), pajamas, and black socks (any number desired); to leave my car at home (no problem, I didn't own one), and warned that "liberty, if any, would be restricted to week ends."

The town of Plattsburg, New York had been the site of an Army post for 130 years. During World War I it had produced second lieutenants for the Army. Since then, the Army had provided summer military training in Plattsburg for thousands of civilians. And now that another war had materialized the Navy had landed in Plattsburg, renaming the old Army post "Camp MacDonough" after a naval hero who defeated the British on nearby Lake Champlain in 1814.

* * * * *

Plattsburg is situated 20 miles from the Canadian border, and when my train puffed into the station on a blustery March afternoon, snow and ice covered the landscape. Buttoning my overcoat, I stepped out of the railroad car to be met by a blast of sub-zero air and a red-faced Navy shore patrolman, who ushered me into the warm station to await the arrival of other officer candidates.

Once all had assembled, we were herded to an open, flat bed truck, where we scrambled for seating on the cold, steel floor. Our escort sheltered himself with the driver in the truck's heated cab. Almost at once there was a grinding of gears and off we sped, while the bitter wind stung our faces and hypothermia threatened. Finally, the truck came to a stop and, shivering, we looked about us at the forbidding precincts of Camp MacDonough.

Notre Dame, Columbia, Northwestern and other institutions of learning had been cranking out midshipmen for some time, but ours would be one of only two classes to be trained at the Plattsburg facility. The Camp's mammoth, snowbound parade ground and surrounding barracks were bleak. The interior of my new home, Building 23, consisted of bathrooms on each floor and large dormitory rooms, sparsely furnished — rows of double decker bunks and foot lockers lined bare hardwood floors, and noisy cast iron radiators rattled away below over-sized, curtainless windows.

Building 23 would house Company K of the regiment of midshipmen ... my company.

Most of the Camp's regiment of midshipmen came from organized V 12 units, and were familiar with the uniform of the Navy enlisted man that we would wear for the first few weeks. My new white underwear of T shirt and boxer shorts ("skivvies") required no introduction. However, I had to learn to swiftly deal with the thirteen buttons securing the front flap of my trousers. I gained new appreciation for the convenience of the humble zipper.

Proper nautical terminology was important in a Navy that had established the use of "port" and "starboard" by a general order in 1846. I learned to refer to the bathroom as the head without feeling self-conscious, and to call my bed a sack, the ceiling the overhead, the stairway a ladder, the wall a bulkhead, and otherwise apply appropriate Navy nomenclature to my surroundings.

I also learned the correct response to bewildering commands, such as: "stand by to give way together" when uttered by our whaleboat coxwain, and "by the left flank march" if ordered by our drill instructor.

* * * * *

On the drill field the Company was divided into two platoons, with the V 12 veterans in an advanced group, and we "civilians" in another. I envied the first platoon their complicated maneuvers, performed with elan as we novices responded awkwardly to the simplest commands. The drill periods were made especially unpleasant by the frigid morning temperatures.

In grammar school there had been "field days" — with foot races and other competition, and prizes for the winners. Happy times. But at Camp MacDonough, "field day" meant preparation for Saturday's inspection. Everyone worked hard — to slack off would be unpopular with the remainder of the Company.

We talked as we worked, and came to know one another better. We would not form lasting friendships — we were too busy for that, and aware that the commissioning ceremony in a few weeks would end our association forever. But meanwhile we were linked by the common, sobering experience of midshipman school, and the mutual uncertainty of the future once we became naval officers. As we labored we exchanged parochial points of view, and in the process learned that Americans did not always think alike on important issues. But we were together in our resolve to win the war.

* * * * *

Midshipmen were allowed to visit Plattsburg on weekends, in limited numbers. The townspeople were hospitable to the Navy pea jackets now in their midst. Churches and the small U.S.O. threw open their doors, and the girls appreciated the law of supply and demand.

Every tenth day we were withdrawn from the classroom to serve on shore patrol or galley detail, where our duties were less cerebral but provided no respite from the 16-hour work days.

Shore patrol meant exposure to frostbite as, unarmed and with black woolen watch caps pulled down over our ears, we guarded the camp's portals against improbable invasion. Galley duty involved dicing onions until our eyes streamed, or scalding our hands in boiling wash water, but there was compensation ... we pilfered pies as they passed through the overheated kitchen.

* * * * *

Almost as soon as we arrived at Plattsburg, word began to circulate that we were destined for amphibious duty, manning landing craft for invasion. Throughout our training the rumor persisted, given credence despite official denials. Camp MacDonough's location on the shore of Lake Champlain was suspicious, with lessons in small boat seamanship a part of the school's curriculum. And we were aware of the very real need for officers to command amphibious craft. We underwent aptitude tests, and were assured that our records were carefully reviewed in the placement process.

My placement interview was brief. A phlegmatic lieutenant (j.g.) from the Bureau of Personnel in Washington made careful notes on lined yellow paper. He asked my duty preference and seemed to sympathize with my ambition to serve on a destroyer in the Pacific.

When notified of our duty assignments a short time prior to graduation, we learned that the rumors were true … most of the regiment would indeed serve in amphibious craft. And thus we came to respect the Navy communication network known as "scuttlebutt." (In the Navy's early days, a ship's drinking water was stored in a wooden cask called a scuttlebutt, the nautical forerunner of the office water cooler. And when sailors gathered at the cask for a drink there was an opportunity to exchange the latest gossip.)

* * * * *

The first hour of Company K's class day was spent in physical training. After breakfast, we marched to a gymnasium occupying the entire second floor of the biggest building at Camp MacDonough. Here future ensigns were subjected to calisthenics by a well-conditioned group of athletic specialists holding the rank of chief petty officer. Perched comfortably on a platform in front of lines of straining midshipmen, they barked out the count for various exercises.

Several sports were offered during the gym class, including boxing. Reluctant pugilists entered the ring and jabbed at each other cautiously while the chief in charge stood outside, futilely shouting "punish yourselves, men." The Camp boxing tournament, which every midshipman was required to enter, entertained him greatly for the few days that it lasted.

We were tested for night-blindness and learned to use our peripheral vision in the dark. Identification of planes and ships was also taught.

Close order drill was easy enough once we had mastered the commands, and our "civilian" platoon soon became as proficient as the V 12 veterans.

* * * * *

Class work was not too demanding except for its considerable volume.

The goal of navigation instruction was to qualify us as pilots in bays and harbors, and also as assistant navigators at sea. The quizzes, distributed in silence, presented more problems than we could reasonably expect to solve in the allotted time. No one was to steal a glance at the questions until the instructor gave the word, and then the race against the clock began. Parallel rulers clacked and dividers stabbed. Perspiration ran, accompanied by muffled profanity.

During a daily ten-minute test on Morse code, we struggled with five-letter code groups. The blinker signals of one of our instructors were occasionally erratic — scuttlebutt had it that he suffered residual stress from bombing attacks in the Pacific. His spasms provided good practice ... we all passed the exam at the conclusion of the course.

* * * * *

A talented midshipman band at Plattsburg Barracks played marches or swing music with equal gusto. Every Wednesday evening the band broadcast a program on the local radio station entitled "Hats Off To The Navy."

Sunday morning church services in the Chapel were well attended. Everyone joined in singing the Navy Hymn — several verses ended prophetically for many of my classmates: "Oh hear us when we cry to Thee, for those in peril on the sea."

We also encountered the "Commando Run," a three-hundred-yard obstacle course. We were expected to negotiate these obstructions in six to eight minutes, and our old nemeses the athletic specialists were alongside to motivate us every step of the way.

* * * * *

So long as winter gripped Lake Champlain, the regiment failed to appreciate the beauty of upper New York State's resort country. It was bitterly cold. Inadequately protected by the hip-length pea jacket of the enlisted man, we were stung by the biting wind off the lake. Early in the morning, lined up on the shore outside the mess hall, we watched the sun rise like a great red ball from somewhere in Vermont. It failed to generate any appreciable warmth at that early hour, and we were shivering when we stumbled in for breakfast.

When spring was in full bloom at home in Missouri, there was a snowstorm at the Camp. Long after the snow disappeared and the ice on the lake melted, Lake Champlain remained too cold for swimming. However, one spring day we looked about us and realized that this was now a pleasant place where the tempo of camp moderated in concert with nature. And while we still counted the days until we were to be commissioned, an unpleasant grind became more tolerable.

Occasionally we paraded on the drill field in our dress blue midshipman uniforms, complete with white gloves and spotless rifles … snappy but uncomfortable. As spring wore on and a hot sun beat down, we were cautioned to consume salt pills and not to lock our knees while standing in ranks. Despite these precautions, men sometimes grew faint. Contributing factors were innoculations against diseases that we might be exposed to after graduation. These assaults by the medical corpsmen preceded the Saturday parades and increased the toll on the drill field. The V 12 men had already undergone this ordeal, so it was the "civilians" who tended to collapse during parades.

CHAPTER SEVEN

Engaging the Enemy

THE WAR WENT ON without us.

After extensive training including lessons in celestial navigation while flying above the Atlantic Ocean — mostly at night out of Miami, Florida in Pan American flying boats — Fred Olander was commissioned a second lieutenant on April 21, 1944. Although his training appeared to be preparation for service in the Pacific Theatre, he was sent to Great Britain as a B-17 navigator and the only water he would cross was the English Channel, in broad daylight.

Lieutenant Olander became a part of the American Eighth Air Force:

"The Eighth Air Force was one of the great fighting forces in all the history of warfare. It had the best equipment and the best men, all but a handful of whom were civilian Americans, educated and willing to fight for their country and a cause they understood was in doubt .. freedom. It's what made World War II special." (page 78) *MY War*, Andy Rooney, Public Affairs, N.Y.,N.Y.

* * * * *

The repaired USS MacKenzie was near Anzio, Italy in May 1944, providing supplies and fire support for American troops pinned down on the Anzio beach by six Nazi divisions. While there, the crew witnessed a natural explosion that dwarfed the battle's shot and shell:

"The Naples bay was our base, and as the ship history shows, we were anchored there and witnessed the Mt. Vesuvius eruption. Omitted from the history is the fact that, as we watched, some two to three inches of very fine lava dust accumulated on our ships, and all exposed guns and mechanical equipment had to be disassembled and cleaned. No one thought about weighing anchor and moving out of the bay." Albert C. Bean, Jr.

* * * * *

Second Lieutenant Henry W. Bloch also joined the Eighth Air Force as a B-17 navigator. Given a choice of assignments among pilot, navigator and bombadier, Henry opted for pilot training but was overruled by his mother.

Part of the training involved firing machine gun bullets from an open-cockpit plane ... Henry qualified as an expert.

Upon completing his training, Lieutenant Bloch sailed for England and the war aboard the Queen Mary. Upon arrival, he was sent to a base in Horham. When Henry entered the Nissen hut that would be his home, he found Air Force personnel stuffing a duffel bag with the belongings of a flier who had not returned from a bombing mission over Germany. Henry was assigned his bunk.

Henry was part of a ten-man crew who named their B-17 "Heaven Can Wait." The first mission of the "Heaven Can Wait" took the plane to Berlin, Germany's most heavily defended target. Once the plane reached its target and started its bomb run, it could not take evasive action and three of its four engines were shot out. After the bomb run, and losing altitude, the plane dropped out of formation and returned to Horham alone. It completed the ten-hour mission and sputtered to a stop out of gas. Thus ended Henry's first mission ... there would be many more.

On D Day the "Heaven Can Wait" flew three missions.

> "They were easy runs, a short flight over the English Channel followed by release of the bomb load without even reaching the beach ... because the bombs fell forward. The sight of the armada of thousands of ships was unforgettable." Henry Bloch

* * * * *

In the South Pacific, Frank Cortelyou's *Log* briefly acknowledged the far away D Day event: "Heard about landing in Europe."

The need to supply the Army's requirements after D Day made heavy demands on amphibious craft. Earl Stark was now an ensign aboard the newly commissioned USS LST 572, landing support troops, cargo and ammunition on Normandy's Omaha Beach and later at Brittany's Michele-en-Gaeve.

Red Callaway, promoted to captain, landed on Omaha Beach with his truck company shortly after D Day. Soon they would be part of the famed Red Ball Express, supplying General George S. Patton Jr.'s fast-moving tanks as they crossed France on their way to Germany.

Dave Robinson, in England since January 1944, was also a part of George Patton's Third Army and landed on Normandy's Utah Beach just a month after D Day. He was assigned to the 39th Evacuation Hospital which over the next year relocated fifteen times as it followed the war:

> "We moved in and out of France, Belgium, Luxembourg and Germany. We moved to keep in proximity to the fighting units. We were usually about 10 - 20 miles from the front line, which gave us the authority for wearing five combat ribbons. We weren't actually fighting, but we were in the combat zone.

> "Our troops were extremely busy caring for the wounded. There were days when I operated as much as fourteen hours or more, usually under safe conditions. We were sometimes operating in tents in the field, or we took over buildings in small towns." David W. Robinson.

* * * * *

Kansas Citian David L. Smart, commissioned a second lieutenant and bombardier in December of 1943, went on his first mission on June 26, 1949 — substituting with a crew that had lost their bombardier. Upon their safe return, the crew told Dave that it had been their thirteenth mission but they had refrained earlier from disclosing the unlucky number to him.

Dave rejoined his own crew for their flight number one on June 29, flying a plane that had been badly damaged on the previous day's mission. Number one proved to be unlucky ... their first mission was their last. After releasing its bombs over a German target, the plane had to drop out of formation and the crew bailed out over Holland. Dave was captured.

Lieutenant Smart was confined briefly in a small prison in Holland, where his German captors gave him a copy of *Winnie the Pooh* to read. He came to know the children's classic by heart. He was also on the receiving end of an Americab bombing raid one night ... the explosions lit his cell but did no damage to the prison.

Dave was later sent to a prison camp in Germany — Stalag Luft One — where he remained until released by Russian troops the following May.

The Tuskegee Airmen, and Herman Johnson, moved from North Africa to Sicily, and in the summer of 1944 were established in southern Italy. They began to fly the newly available P-51 Mustangs on their bomber escort missions and, wanting the bomber crews and the German Luftwaffe to know who they were, painted the P-51 tails bright red. The initial reactions of the mostly white bomber crews were hostile, but as the Airmen's reputation grew for tenacious defense of bombers, they were requested as escorts by bomber crews who began to call them "Red Tail Angels." The Red Tails flew 200 bomber escort missions against heavily defended targets and never lost a bomber to enemy fighters. "We were a crack outfit." Herman Johnson.

* * * * *

Other P-51 pilots based in southern Italy were the members of the American Beagle Squadron, the 2nd Fighter Squadron of the 52nd Fighter Group. They were joined on August 15, 1944, by nine new pilots including Kansas Citian Thomas Conway Leary. Commissioned a second lieutenant on March 12, 1944, Conway Leary had trained on P-47s but now he would fly the coveted P-51.

* * * * *

Half the world away, the Marianas campaign was launched with costly amphibious landings on the islands of Saipan, Tinian and Guam. Bob Hanger was one of the Marianas combatants, landing on Saipan on June 15, and Tinian on July 24.

It was from Tinian that the Enola Gay flew, carrying the atomic bomb, to keep a date with history over Hiroshima.

The Tinian operation also involved the Colorado and Bill Woodson:

"The trip over from Saipan was downright peaceful for the troops, but marked by a determined naval bombardment of Tinian town as part of the deception. The battleship Colorado (with Ensign William Hamilton Woodson, an old M.U. roommate of mine aboard) was involved in a shoot out with one or more Japanese mountain guns up in the hills. We watched while the great ship prowled up and down the coast looking for the culprits and taking a succession of hits. The enemy firepower wasn't sufficient to cause the battle wagon any significant damage, but casualties were heavy. Woodson, by the way, wasn't hurt.

"I didn't get to see the end of the duel owing to debarkation for the landing which changed my position from spectator to participant." *Who's gonna live?* Robert C. Hanger, 1997, p.38.

Aboard the Colorado, the crew obeyed the ship's directives for "First Aid in Battle," a grim statement of priorities:

"THE WATER-TIGHT INTEGRITY OF THE SHIP, REGARDLESS OF WOUNDED, MUST BE PRESERVED. This means that wounded cannot be taken to battle dressing stations for treatment until after the battle is over, or there is a lull.

"FIRE POWER, AS DELIVERED BY BATTERIES OF THE SHIP, REGARDLESS OF WOUNDED, MUST BE MAINTAINED. This means that men necessary for manning guns must be treated promptly and returned to their stations if possible. It also means that while needed to keep your gun functioning you may not leave it to care for the wounded."

Another spectator of the Colorado duel was Allen Woodson whose New Orleans, like the Colorado, took part in a number of Pacific island campaigns.

* * * * *

Gordon Robertson, and the Hornet, part of Task Group 58.3 under Rear Admiral J.J.(Jocko) Clark, had participated in strikes against Palau, Truk (the "Gibraltar of the Pacific"), and other Japanese strongholds and on France's D Day sortied from Majuro for the invasion of the Mariana islands. Bombing Squadron Two first hit Guam, a major island in the chain, on June 12. A few days after the initial Guam assault, a pilot with a brother in the Marines asked Gordon and others to join him in looking for his brother ashore. The search was unsuccessful and the pilots returned to the beach, hoping to find transportation back to the Hornet. But the only things afloat were the warships anchored well offshore, including the Hornet.

"After some time, while we were trying to decide what to do next, Admiral Jocko Clark's barge came to the pier. The coxwain, there to pick up the admiral, said that he would try to return us to the ship. Soon the admiral and three of his staff came to the pier from exploring ashore. He wondered what we were doing there and how we intended to return to the Hornet. When told that we planned to catch the next mail boat, his response left no doubt that he thought we had lost our minds.

"At the coxwain's request, Admiral Clark agreed to let us return with him. The barge could take all but three of us. With the admiral's permission the barge would return for the remaining three. 'Very well,' said Admiral Clark, 'but come hell or high water, we're getting underway at 1700.' The coxwain did return the last of us to the ship just as the Hornet was weighing anchor and the last of the gangway was being brought up. We rode the barge as it was hoisted aboard while the Hornet got underway.

"We almost joined the Marines that day!" Gordon Robertson.

The attacks by the Hornet's Air Group continued:

"On 19 June, while in a dive bombing attack on an AA emplacement, I saw that the bomber just ahead of me in the dive had been hit by large caliber AA fire. The plane, smoking, pulled out of his dive and headed for the harbor nearby. Shortly after clearing the beach the rear seat gunner bailed out. Then the pilot stood in the cockpit to follow. I flew next to him and since no fire was visible, I motioned for the pilot to sit down. If he could continue for just a short distance, we would be out of the range of shore fire and his chance of rescue would be greatly improved. The plane did not burn and stayed airborne. I motioned for him to join up on me and led him back to the Hornet." Gordon Robertson.

The plane had no flaps, a large hole in the right wing, and only one wheel down, but the pilot brought it aboard safely. Although his chute opened, the crewman who bailed out so close to the beach was never found.

Later in June, during the First Battle of the Philippine Sea, Hornet bombers bagged a 30,000-ton Japanese carrier.

* * * * *

Second Lieutenant David Douglas Duncan, combat photographer, worked his way through the Solomon Islands and the Western Pacific, often outrunning his supply line:

"Although based with the Marines' only photo-bomber air squadron at Espiritu Santo in the New Hebrides, his orders from the South Pacific Combat Air Transport Command (SCAT) were broad and far-ranging. He had access to most military bases and operations and was able to document all aspects of SCAT's operations throughout the many island bases covering the Pacific Theater.

"In one dramatic instance he saw action with Fijian guerrillas fighting behind Japanese lines on Bougainville Island." *David Douglas Duncan: One Life, A Photographic Odyssey,* Harry Ransom Humanities Research Center, The University of Texas at Austin.

On Bougainville, the tables were turned when photographer Duncan's picture was taken by a young Navy lieutenant destined to achieve fame in another line of work: Richard M. Nixon.

* * * * *

Jim Kemper was sent to the South Pacific as a replacement officer, landing at Port Moresby, New Guinea. He was assigned to the 8th Cavalry of the 1st Cavalry Division, a regular Army division that had seen a great deal of action. In June, Jim received a letter from his brother David, with Headquarters Company of the Army's IV Corps in the European Theater:

"Got your letter of March 3 a little while ago and today received a letter from Pappy saying you are now with the 1st Cavalry Div. Guess you will run into some honest to God fighting … so better keep that 6'2" close to the ground. Has your marksmanship improved any? I am still fighting it out along the chow line and am doing about as well as can be expected. The psychology of war is a queer thing. Your mind tells you that it is a sucker's game to go to the front — wars are silly and dead heros are dead for a long time — but other people go, it *is* an acid test and you wonder if you can pass it. You read about the Commando Kelly boys, and ... first thing you know you want to go. A funny business. I hope this war ends soon but I don't think it will. That Japan war should drag on for several years. Fondly, Dave."

CHAPTER EIGHT

To the Pacific

AT CAMP MACDONOUGH, the day arrived when we received our duty assignments. We stood in ranks and waited tensely for our orders, distributed in sealed envelopes and opened with nervous fingers. Revolutionary War naval hero John Paul Jones once declared his intention to "go in harm's way." In the classroom the words had been inspirational, but now reality confronted us.

While most of the regiment were scheduled for amphibious craft, replacing the casualties of the Normandy landings and the Pacific island assaults, a handful of us received different orders. Mine directed me to report to the Commander-in-Chief of the Pacific Fleet "for active duty, and for further assignment to such general duties as may be required." There was no explanation of why I had been singled out for special treatment, but I was spared from amphibious duty, and en route to the West Coast I would have seven days at home.

Then came graduation day at Camp MacDonough. We had been wearing an officer's uniform for several weeks, the anchors on our lapels proclaiming midshipman status — officers inchoate. Now, however, on the 27th of June, 1944, we exchanged those anchors for a gold stripe on our sleeve and a gold bar on our collar. The threat of bilging out of midshipman school was but a memory. We marched to the parade ground for the last time, certified "ninety day wonders" (actually 113 days, but who had been counting?). The sun was far different than the feeble orb that had stared red-eyed at us in early March. Now it blazed away, determined to make us forget its earlier shortcomings. Before the ceremony was well underway, the audience of parents and friends sweltered in the heat, and our starched, detachable shirt collars wilted. But all discomfort was forgotten in celebration as the graduation exercises came to an end. Then Company K dispersed to pack and leave Camp MacDonough. Few of us would ever meet again. Another midshipman class had graduated, and a new crop of ensigns was embarking upon the great adventure of World War II.

* * * * *

I celebrated the Fourth of July at home. That day, Jim Kemper led his first combat patrol — on the island of Manus, one of the Admiralty Islands. Manus had been wrested from the Japanese but there were still many enemy soldiers at large on the island. The Japanese warrior code, bushido, glorified a soldier's death and Japanese soldiers carried field codes admonishing them to die rather than "incur the shame" of capture. Consequently, the Japanese stragglers on Manus fought to the death and American patrols took no prisoners. Every Independence Day, Jim Kemper recalls the July 4, 1944 fighting on Manus Island.

* * * * *

After a few notable days' leave, I was delivered by my parents to Kansas City's bustling Union Station. Wartime travelers packed the monumental terminal building, filling the long wooden benches, patronizing the Fred Harvey Restaurant and assorted shops and stands, and passing through the doors leading to and from the train platforms below. Excited greetings and tearful farewells were exchanged beneath the Station's great clock, as uniformed service personnel came and went.

The war was much in evidence in the great rail center where the number of daily trains was swollen by hundreds of extra troop cars. Throngs of soldiers stopped over in the Station between trains, and volunteers contributed many hours to the Traveler's Aid Society and the city's servicemen's centers.

A booth in the Union Station sold war bonds ... in one war bond drive, Kansas Citians purchased $128 million worth. Sally Tourtellot was asked to promote the sale of defense stamps at another Station location and to wear a uniform — she wore the only one she had, her high school drum majorette's uniform.

* * * * *

For my journey to the West Coast I reserved a roomette on the Santa Fe Railroad's celebrated "Chief," the ultimate luxury in transcontinental travel. Both parents accompanied me to the train platform and we parted beside the Pullman car's metal steps — Dad, who had gone to France with the Marine Corps in response to President Wilson's call to "make the world safe for democracy," hid his qualms behind a proud smile, but Mom was betrayed by the tears in her eyes. Then I boarded the train, found my room and settled down for the ride to San Francisco.

I was wearing my dress blue uniform, and looked every inch a brand new Navy ensign. I had squandered part of my $150 uniform allowance on a splendid white outfit of palm beach material that I had packed as well. Fortunately I also brought along the drab, battleship gray uniform which, by directive from Admiral Ernest J. King, Navy Commander-in-Chief, was replacing khaki as the naval officer's cotton work clothing.

The trip was pleasant, on a train whose many amenities attracted passengers of note. Admiral Chester W. Nimitz had ridden the Santa Fe Chief in December 1941, on his way to Pearl Harbor to assume command of the battered Pacific Fleet.

I changed trains at Barstow, and finally reached San Francisco at 0130 on July 12. When I immediately reported for transportation to Pacific Fleet headquarters in Hawaii, my devotion to duty was not appreciated by a sleepy Navy yeoman. I was sent to the Franciscan Hotel for the night.

* * * * *

The following afternoon I moved to the Alexander Hamilton Hotel, a naval officers' B.O.Q. (Bachelor Officers' Quarters), to await the trip to Hawaii. The hotel's occupants all seemed to be waiting — for orders, for their ships to arrive, or for a ride to their duty stations, and meanwhile merely for time to pass. I discovered that there is a great deal of waiting in a war. On their advice I shipped home the palm beach whites, purchased a reliable wrist watch at Fort Mason, and at the Navy's Treasure Island facility obtained identifying dog tags (#370093) ominously listing my blood type (A). I also passed a required swimming test at the Armory, and invested in a supply of six cent airmail stamps for overseas use (regular mail was three cents, and post card stamps cost a penny).

Every morning I attended a compulsory class in a nautical subject of my choosing, at the Twelfth Naval District headquarters ... a stratagem to keep transient naval officers on a leash amid the temptations of "Baghdad on the Bay." It was also necessary to maintain contact with the B.O.Q. for travel orders. Otherwise my time was my own to investigate San Francisco.

There were many uniforms on the streets of San Francisco ... navy blue was easily the dominant color. And one evening, as several of us dined in a downtown restaurant, a couple about the age of my parents sent complimentary wine to our table. I suspected that our benefactors had a son somewhere in the Navy. However, the culinary delights of this beautiful city were expensive for a newly commissioned ensign of limited means. And since I was not yet twenty-one years of age, some notable watering places were off limits to me — such as the fabled "Top of the Mark" bar atop the Mark Hopkins Hotel.

CHAPTER NINE

Aloha!

ON JULY 15, 1944, my twenty-first birthday anniversary, I received orders to report to the Port Director, San Pedro, California. A San Francisco newspaper informed readers that on the same day in the year of our Lord 1099, Christian Crusaders had recaptured Jerusalem from the Muslims. My own war against the infidels was just beginning.

The following day I traveled by rail to San Pedro. Upon arrival I was directed to LST 609 for transportation to the headquarters of the Commander-in-Chief of the Pacific Fleet. Once aboard I was welcomed by the ship's commanding officer. We soon weighed anchor and my first sea voyage began. Our destination was Pearl Harbor, where most of the damage sustained on December 7, 1941, had long since been repaired.

As a passenger on a small naval vessel, I had only to stay out of the way of the ship's crew and not drink all of the coffee. (This trip introduced me to the Navy's "joe," a stimulant reputed to be of such strength and consistency that a coin would float on its surface.) However, as a neophyte sailor, I enjoyed all of my new experiences — the fresh salt air, the sparkling blue water, the phosphorescent wake of the blacked out LST under a starlit sky, even the motion of the ship. I had been blessed with a cast iron stomach, and after an initial queasiness had no symptoms of mal de mer.

The gold emblems on some of the officers' hats bore a greenish tinge, a patina caused by repeated exposure to ocean spray — indicia of an "old salt" among the ship's company. New ensigns were not above hastening the process by overnight applications of sea water.

The initials "LST" were an abbreviation for "Landing Ship Tank," the ungainly flat-nosed craft designed to transport armored vehicles to invasion sites. Its dominant feature was a cavernous tank deck, and it was capable of grounding and discharging tanks or trucks on beaches. Many of my Plattsburg classmates were destined for amphibious assaults aboard such ships, and I examined the 609 with interest.

LSTs were nicknamed "Large Slow Targets," and our trip to Pearl required some ten days to negotiate. But there was plenty of reading material, the food in the mess was good, and I caught up on my sleep. And finally, on July 26, we reached Hawaii.

* * * * *

The arrival of LST 609 at Pearl coincided with that of the cruiser USS Baltimore. The latter was flying the presidential flag, signifying the presence aboard of President Franklin D. Roosevelt. As a result, the entrance of our own modest man-of-war into the harbor was delayed. Meanwhile when the president's ship drew alongside the pier, a number of admirals from the headquarters of Admiral Chester W. Nimitz, Commander-in-Chief, Pacific Fleet, were waiting to board it. The scene was described in Ronald H. Spector's *Eagle Against The Sun* (published by Vintage Books, a division of Random House, New York), as follows:

33

"At their head was Nimitz's chief of staff, Admiral Charles H. McMorris. 'Right face' ordered McMorris — and two of the admirals promptly faced left, much to the delight of the Baltimore's sailors. Seldom had they witnessed such a graphic confirmation of their private views on the competence of 'the top brass.' " (p. 417).

We missed the ceremony at the pier, but while we waited outside the harbor a vast fleet of war planes flew in spectacular, thunderous waves above us. The show was for FDR, but our vantage point was just as good as his.

The Baltimore was preceded by a plane from Australia, carrying General Douglas MacArthur to a meeting with the President and Admiral Nimitz.

* * * * *

The following day I reported to the Cincpac Officers' Pool, to await assignment. "Cincpac" was the Navy's acronym for "Commander-in-Chief, Pacific Fleet."

My ensign's commission was exactly one month old. As I waited, I continued to hope for destroyer duty — knowing nothing about destroyers but harboring a vague notion that the Navy's real sailors were to be found aboard its "tin cans."

A day or so later, I stood admiring the pink splendor of Honolulu's Royal Hawaiian Hotel on Waikiki Boulevard when a limousine drew up, bearing the President of the United States. The famous hotel was being used for rest and recreation by Navy submariners and aviators, after duty in the combat zones of the Pacific theater. When the president emerged from the car his trademark cigarette holder was at its customary jaunty angle, but I was dismayed to see how crippled he was — throughout his presidency, photographers had engaged in a benign conspiracy to conceal the ravages of poliomyelitis from the American people.

Shortly we were addressed by a voice familiar from countless radio broadcasts … the president's "fireside chats" had projected a reassuring father-image to a nation stunned first by economic catastrophe and then by the trauma of a great war. Now his Honolulu audience consisted primarily of young pilots who had earlier listened to those chats in the sanctuary of their own homes. Aged beyond their years and far from familiar firesides, they were veterans of the previous month's "Marianas Turkey Shoot" .. flying from American carriers they had decimated Japanese carrier-based air power, as a prelude to invasion of the Mariana islands.

* * * * *

On July 21, while LST 609 was en route to Hawaii, FDR had been nominated for a fourth term as President of the United States, with Senator Harry S. Truman of Missouri as his vice presidential running mate. The election would be in November, less than four months away. Roosevelt's trip to Hawaii may have been politically motivated — a much photographed meeting by FDR, the consummate politician, with Admiral Nimitz and General Douglas MacArthur would do no harm in an election year. But it also provided an opportunity to adjudicate an Olympian dispute; to wit, whether to strike next at the Philippines as urged by MacArthur or the island of Formosa as favored by Nimitz.

Leaping across thousands of square miles of Pacific Ocean to Formosa was a continuation of the island-hopping strategy conceived and put in motion by Nimitz. Under that concept, enemy island strongholds were to be bypassed, deprived of supplies, and forced to surrender without the bloodshed resulting from frontal assaults on heavily defended positions.

The admiral argued that an invasion of the Philippines would be unnecessary … neutralizing the archipelago's air bases would be sufficient. (Robert W. Bergstrom, March 1999 issue of *World War II)*

However, MacArthur was committed to a return to the Philippines ("I shall return") and the president accepted his proposal. The Joint Chiefs of Staff later acquiesced in a costly frontal assault upon the Philippine island of Leyte, as I would learn in a few months.

* * * * *

For several days nothing was required of me but to report daily to the officers' pool for assignment. The rest of the time I was free to enjoy Hawaii.

Then a United States territory, Hawaii would not achieve statehood until 1959. Separated from California by several thousand miles of Pacific ocean, it was unlike anything the mainland had to offer. The dramatic island scenery, the fragrance and brilliance of its vegetation, the warmth and tolerance of its handsome, multi-racial population, its romantic music and soft tradewinds, all had the allure of Paradise for the servicemen who passed through there in the course of the war.

CHAPTER TEN

CINCPAC

ON AUGUST 10, I received my duty assignment — the Cincpac operations office where I would be a plotting officer, whatever that was. Perversely, I stated my preference for a destroyer … perhaps to "go in harm's way" and compensate for my tardy entry into the war. But the discussion ended abruptly when a lieutenant commander told me: "I don't really give a damn whether you like it or not," and sent me to Cincpac.

I soon realized that I was very lucky to be attached to the Cincpac staff.

Cincpac headquarters on Makalapa Hill was a concrete bastion, where the most impressive figures were not the top brass frequenting the premises, but the tall Marines who comprised the security force. Known to us as the "palace guard," they wore special caps somewhat larger than regulation and their starched uniforms were always immaculate and wrinkle-free, a characteristic that required a great deal of effort. They climbed on chairs to put on their pants, and they remained standing in the back of a truck en route to their duty stations, all in order to avoid creases.

I was introduced to the duties and responsibilities of my new job. My subterranean, bomb-proof work station was called "flag plot." I had top secret clearance, and was privy to almost every development of any consequence in the Pacific Theater. A constant flow of secret dispatches enabled the denizens of flag plot to follow the Navy's war, and keep track of every seagoing Navy unit in the Pacific.

I was told that a hand-cranked "scramble" telephone in flag plot connected to a corresponding secure instrument at Nimitz's bedside, but never had occasion to use it.

* * * * *

Before the war, Uncle Sam winked at the presence in Hawaii of numerous prostitutes. They posed little threat to the morals of hardened professional military. But informative letters home from young draftees and volunteers were another matter, and many of the women were removed Stateside.

The evacuation did not abolish Honolulu's red light district. "Flaming Mamie," a prosperous survivor of the clean-up, introduced assembly-line efficiency to the oldest profession. Her marketing efforts were constant: a young Cincpac sailor, dispatched to post warnings against divulging classified information ("Loose Lips Sink Ships"), reported on his return that he had been received by Mamie with a friendly pat on the fanny and an invitation to return when off duty.

Mamie's patron's were checked for venereal disease … an intimate examination known in the armed forces as a "short arm inspection."

* * * * *

I took up residence in a Cincpac B.O.Q. with two naval officers, Dick Dilworth and Gil Clee, as roommates. They were congenial and considerate, and I appreciated my good fortune.

37

My roommates wore khaki uniforms, not Admiral King's somber gray. "Admiral Nimitz prefers khaki," they told me. During a visit by King to the largely khaki-clad Cincpac headquarters, one of his entourage returned the salute of a newly-minted ensign sporting a suit of grays tailored for him in San Francisco, and offered "congratulations on wearing the uniform of the day." However, khaki remained king at Cincpac.

I continued to wear the gray uniform issued to Camp MacDonough's graduates ... no one insisted that I invest in a new wardrobe.

Our B.O.Q., occupied by more or less permanent staff officers, was tranquil; the transient billets were not. Their occupants had often been at sea for many months and would return to the alternately boring and hazardous existence of seagoing sailors, with only a brief respite in Hawaii to sustain them. Consequently, transient B.O.Q.s were rollicking places, filled with the sounds of crap and poker games and of revelers noisily returning to their quarters.

* * * * *

Admiral Nimitz' house was up the hill from our B.O.Q., on the rim of Makalapa crater. There was a swimming pool on the admiral's premises where, after standing the mid-watch, junior officers some-times sneaked a "skinny dip" before breakfast and bed. If the admiral was aware of the trespassers, he said nothing.

Lieutenant H.G. Kaufman of Kansas City, now a seasoned Communications Duty Officer, had served on the Cincpac staff ever since his arrival at Pearl Harbor as a brand-new ensign almost two years earlier. The staff was much smaller then, and for a time the very junior Hal Kaufman occupied a house on Makalapa. He was invited to join Admiral Nimitz on several social occasions. As was the case with all of the young men on the Cincpac staff, Hal admired the Admiral greatly.

Until his house was confiscated by higher rank, Hal enjoyed the good life on Makalapa hill:

"For dances at the Sub Base our band leader was Artie Shaw. Our tennis instructor was Bobbie Riggs. We played poker at the house with Oswald Jacobi, also with leftenants Jones and Hughes from HMS Victorious. Some of us enjoyed dinner on their carrier with those British officers. The liquor availability there was noticeably different than on our ships ... Every morning out the window a rainbow began its day ... Up by the rainbow was Aiea Naval Hospital (now gone) behind which a trail began through the mountains. Armed with the mandatory heavy .45 I often walked there among the small orchids on the trees."

Hal Kaufman.

CHAPTER ELEVEN

Worldwide War

IN AUGUST, the MacKenzie provided gunfire support for an Allied assault on the coast of Southern France, in the process shelling a German fort and receiving in return eleven near misses from enemy gun batteries. On August 27, sixteen German soldiers from the fort's garrison commandeered a small boat, rowed out to the MacKenzie, and surrendered.

* * * * *

In September, Tom Thompson arrived at Mohonbari in India's Assam Valley. Now an Army Air Corps pilot, Lieutenant Thompson was a member of the Air Transport Command assigned to "fly the Hump" in the China, Burma, India (CBI) Theater of Operations — sometimes referred to as the forgotten theater of the war.

The "Hump" was the Himalayan Mountains, towering as high as 23,000 feet along the border between China and Burma. The only supply route to Nationalist Chinese troops fighting the Japanese was the Burma Road … a winding, unpaved road that began at the seaport of Rangoon in Burma and ended in Kunming, China, crossing the rugged Hump en route.

India was connected to the Burma Road by a road constructed through the Ledo Pass by Army Engineers assisted by glider troops, the famed Merrill's Marauders, all under the command of Joseph ("Vinegar Joe") Stillwell. Supplies for China were transported to the Ledo Road over the Bengal and Assam Railway, a primitive railroad that crossed difficult, mountainous terrain. The B & A's director of operations was its Trainmaster, Captain William N. Deramus.

An article in a Lowell, Indiana newspaper described the railroad and its contribution to the war effort:

> "Most of the railroad men in India are serving with units of the Military Railway Service on the meter gauge Bengal and Assam Railway … The road was originally built to fulfill the peacetime requirements of the Assam tea planters. Now it is one of the most important supply arteries for American and allied troops.
>
> "A large proportion of the war material destined for China goes over the railroad from Calcutta to depots in Assam; from there it is flown over the Hump by transport planes.
>
> "G.I. railroaders in India have worked under rough conditions, at jungle and mountain outposts, and through monsoon rains. They have done a transportation job unequalled in history." *Lowell Tribune*, August 16, 1945, page 2.

The Air Transport Command, supplementing the Burma Road supply effort, made hazardous daily Hump airlifts. Tom Thompson's ATC plane was the C-46 Commando, affectionately dubbed "Dumbo" after Walt Disney's flying elephant because of its great size.

Television's Andy Rooney undertook a Hump flight in a Dumbo:

"... I climbed aboard a C-46 for a flight over the Himalayas — known simply as 'The Hump.' I sat almost alone in a bucket seat on the airplane, with supplies of all kinds crowding in around me. It was known to be a dangerous flight and I wasn't made any easier by the graffiti someone had crayoned on the inside sheath of the plane right behind my seat:

"THIS IS A THING YOU DON'T SEE OFTEN
TWO ENGINES MOUNTED ON A COFFIN."

My War, supra, p.290

* * * * *

By now Frank Cortelyou was on Banika Island, one of the Russell Group in the Solomons, and here he had a reunion with old friend David Douglas Duncan, who of necessity had become an accomplished scrounger:

"Mon. Aug.7 ... Had the surprise of my life when Duncan appeared in the yard. Had been to Guadalcanal and heard we were here ... Sure glad to see him. We really did some gossiping. As usual he is making the breaks for himself and the war is being very profitable from his photographic viewpoint. Has traveled all over the islands ... Is staying a couple of days. Tues. Aug 8 ... I showed him around a bit — though he saw too many things he would like to swipe ... Wed. Aug 9. Took Dave over to air strip. His plane took off about 9 p.m. He made quite a haul while here ... Got him a flashlight and some extra batteries, transparent tape, couple of rolls of screen wire ... also a used pair of shorts ..." *Personal Log*, supra.

* * * * *

Gordon Robertson's dive bomber squadron was in the thick of things.

After the Marianas campaign, Vice Admiral Mark Mitscher, Commander of Task Force 58, came aboard the Hornet to honor the ship and, in a memorable ceremony, conferred over 200 medals on the ship's airmen.

There followed more battles for the Hornet, including strikes against the Palau Islands, the Philippines, the Moluccas, then back to the Central Philippines. The month of September, with its continuous activity and destructive raids, greatly increased the number of Jap flags on the Hornet's scoreboard — a scoreboard kept on the flight deck's island.

By this time, the bomber squadron was running out of SB2Cs and a third of the pilots, including Robertson, were using F6F Hellcats as fighter bombers.

The Hornet steamed up the coast of Luzon and launched attacks on enemy vessels, installations and airfields in and around Manila Bay where Gordon Robertson sank a Japanese ship and Bombing Two helped leave the Bay a harbor of sunken hulks:

"On September 21, I was part of a strike group that made a pre-dawn launch to fly across Luzon to Manila Bay to attack, shortly after sunrise, vessels in the Bay. The Bay was filled with targets, and after making so many runs on airfields and associated AA guns, seeing all those ships brought joy to the heart of a bomber pilot.

"As I crossed the edge of the Bay I saw a tanker which was putting up some AA fire. The Hellcat had six 50 caliber machine guns and was a formidable weapon. I made a strafing attack on the ship and, as I passed over at 300 feet, it exploded and I flew through the smoke and flames with no ill effect." Gordon Robertson.

The Manila Bay action brought to an end Bombing Squadron Two's phase of Gordon Robertson's war:

"Upon completion of its deployment in the Pacific (last attack occurred on 24 September 1944), the surviving squadron members returned to the United States for thirty days leave and assignment to new duty." Gordon Robertson.

* * * * *

Arthur J. Doyle had left law school in Boston to enlist in the Navy's V 5 program, and in May 1944 was commissioned an ensign and naval aviator. He was assigned to a squadron of F4Us. The distinctive gull-winged Corsairs had been banned from Navy carriers because of excessive landing accidents, and Art's squadron was chosen to demonstrate that, with properly trained pilots, the aircraft could be returned to carrier duty. Art led an eight-plane performance in a Florida demonstration that convinced Navy brass to reinstate the Corsair aboard carriers.

Designated VBF-89 (V = Carrier, B = Bomber, F = Fighter), Doyle's F4U group was assigned to the USS Antietem, a new carrier. Upon the ship's completion, and following a Caribbean shakedown cruise, the Antietem sailed to Pearl Harbor's Ford Island.

* * * * *

Wallace M. Burger, a V-12 graduate of Westminster College in Fulton, Missouri, was assigned to midshipman school at Wellesley College in Massachusetts. Upon being commissioned an ensign in September 1944, he was ordered to report to the light cruiser USS Birmingham, then operating somewhere in the Pacific … part of Task Force 38 engaged in air strikes against Japanese island positions in the Philippines, the Palau group, and later Formosa and Okinawa.

Chasing the Birmingham, Burger traveled to Pearl Harbor in style on the USS Wisconsin, sharing its empty admiral's quarters with other transient Navy officers. In Hawaii he searched for transportation to Ulithi, a Pacific atoll serving as a giant fleet anchorage, where he hoped to catch up with his ship. He finally caught a ride on the Ocelot, a fleet oiler that departed from Pearl Harbor at a very deliberate eleven knots per hour.

* * * * *

On October 14, Conway Leary became a POW. His description of the events of that day is set out in *The American Beagle Squadron*, 1987, The Lexington Press, Lexington, Massachusetts, at page 282:

"As we approached the target area we were a little north of the airfield that was to be strafed … Jack Beard and I were the first planes to attack. We both fired on a line of enemy aircraft that were parked facing us and perpendicular to our line of flight …

"I hit one and it blew up in a ball of fire. Then I kicked rudder to spray other planes in the line and another one blew up. At the same time I felt a jolt under the engine but kept firing until I went over the line of planes.

"As I joined up with Jack I noticed smoke coming from the engine … I told Jack that I was going to make another pass, figuring that if my plane had been hit I might as well do as much damage as possible while my plane was still functioning …

"I turned and came back over the field and down the line of planes. I fired and hit one plane and then another, which blew up ..."

Leary started for home, but had to bail out when his engine caught fire. He was picked up by the Germans and finished the war in a prison camp.

CHAPTER TWELVE

Flag Plot

ON OAHU, downtown Honolulu was bright and bustling in the daylight, with servicemen swarming along the thoroughfares and businessmen in panama hats and lightweight suits conducting their affairs much as their mainland counterparts did in San Francisco or Chicago. Curfew cleared the streets, however; it regulated the lives of servicemen and civilians alike. Businessmen went home to their families. And servicemen retreated for the night to Ft. Shafter, or Pearl Harbor, or Camp Catlin, or Hickam Field.

One of the Cincpac admirals sometimes drove down Honolulu's Hotel Street just before the witching hour and collected stray soldiers and sailors who had missed the last bus back to base. He delivered the sailors as close as possible to their respective ships, but soldiers had to be dropped off at the Army posts' main gate. However, as the admiral was heard to say, "soldiers like to walk."

* * * * *

The principal business of Oahu was pursuit of the war against Japan. And the naval conduct of that war was directed from the Makalapa domain of Cincpac. Admiral Nimitz' headquarters building was at the center of the fighting, the calm eye of war's hurricane.

Flag plot was the Navy's nerve center for the entire Pacific Ocean area, and major command decisions were based on the information collected and displayed there.

American submarines were all over the map — sinking shipping, gathering information, landing coastwatchers on hostile islands, and in general advancing the war effort.

On our big flag plot chart we traced the movements of these submarines. Sub contacts in areas where American boats were scheduled to be on patrol were disregarded, but submarines outside those zones were fair game.

Particularly sensitive were unmarked "lanes" used by our subs to travel to and from their bases, established by coordinates carefully drawn on our chart.

Midwatches, at a time (8 p.m. to 4 a.m.) when most of Hawaii was the sleepiest, seemed to produce the busiest communication traffic. One moonlit night a flurry of angry dispatches protested that Army Air Corps B-24s were attacking submarines in protected lanes. Some of those subs had been on "lifeguard" duty, rescuing bomber crews forced to ditch planes damaged in air strikes against the Japanese. The lanes' coordinates had been changed during the day, but the "flying boxcar" pilots had not gotten "the Word."

The senior staff duty officer was asleep on a cot in the operations office. Lieutenant Roland Petering, a former Kansas City banker who was now a Communication Watch Officer, awakened him and explained the emergency. The duty officer, a Navy captain, raised up on one elbow, listened, and then brusquely ordered: "Change the lanes back."

Pete came to flag plot, where I was the plotting officer on duty, and said:

"You and I have to change the submarine lanes for the Pacific Fleet. We had better do it right or we'll be weaving baskets at the naval prison in Newport, Rhode Island for the rest of our lives."

I plotted the changes and Pete notified the submarine fleet commander of the new coordinates. No American subs were sunk, and we were not consigned to Newport.

* * * * *

The great October 1944 Battle of Leyte Gulf, precipitated by Roosevelt's earlier Honolulu decision to invade the Philippine island of Leyte, was followed on our flag plot chart.

The 1st Cavalry Division came ashore at Leyte Gulf's Tacloban. Jim Kemper's platoon landed in the 8th wave at 11:00 a.m.:

"Landing begins 8 a.m. October 20.
"Battleships Mississippi, Maryland, West Virginia.
"9:45 landing craft to beaches.
"Easy landing — no surf — no mines — slight enemy reaction.
"Total casualties Beach Red 50.
"1st Cavalry lands Beach White — Very successful — no opposition.
"MacArthur lands that afternoon. Makes speech on beach."

James M. Kemper Jr.

As far as the general was concerned, only then did the war in the Philippines get underway:

"General MacArthur declared, for purposes of eligibility for the Philippine Liberation Ribbon, that the campaign did not begin until his return. Thus, our Air Group did not qualify for that recognition." Gordon Robertson.

* * * * *

I was on duty in Cincpac's flag plot during these climactic battles. The top brass were already copied on the dispatches flying back and forth, but the pictures on our big chart were worth a thousand words. High-ranking officers looked on as I traced the battle, respectfully elbowing aside the kibitzers. I was recording history while far removed from the flesh and blood heroics reported in the dispatches.

The Japanese navy suffered such losses in the Leyte Gulf engagements that it ceased to be a major factor in the Pacific war.

After nine months in the Aleutians and a new coat of camouflage paint in San Francisco, the Luce shepherded a flock of LSTs to Leyte. There, the Japanese introduced kamikaze suicide planes to the Pacific war and Cliff Jones viewed first hand the appalling new tactic.

Cincpac censorship forbade disclosure of the kamikazes' heavy toll, in the vain hope that this weapon would not be made a regular part of the enemy's arsenal — but the destruction was there for all to see.

* * * * *

On October 24, during the Leyte engagement, a Japanese plane dropped a bomb squarely in the middle of the flight deck of the aircraft carrier Princeton. The Birmingham was dispatched to assist the stricken carrier and was alongside the Princeton when it exploded. The cruiser's casualties were three times those on the carrier — 239 dead, 408 wounded, and 4 missing. The Birmingham was ordered back to San Francisco's Mare Island Navy Base for extensive repairs. Because of the slow speed of the Ocelot, Wally Burger arrived at Ulithi after the explosion and the Birmingham's departure for the West Coast. He spent several weeks as a Ulithi shore patrolman before obtaining transportation back to San Francisco and the Birmingham.

* * * * *

On October 29, ending two years in the South Pacific, Frank Cortelyou recorded his return to the States on a foggy evening: "Under the Golden Gate Bridge at 1835 and were barely able to see it ... still hard to realize we're actually in the USA." *Personal Log*, supra.

* * * * *

The men and women of Dr. Max Berry's 117th Station Hospital arrived at Leyte Gulf on November 19:

"The convoy was a big one and when it came in it had a good bit of attention from the Japanese Air Force. There were dogfights, bombs dropping, explosions and commotion all over the blasted harbor ... One of the unusual things about the air attack was the new Japanese planes called kamikazes. They came in sailing over the water straight at the ships and everybody was shooting at them. Most of them were shot down but when one got away it would dive into some ship and blow the hell out of it. These were the kamikazes that the Japanese had been saving for the time they had to defend their own territory ..." *One Man's WWII*, supra, pp.55-56.

* * * * *

On November 27, in Leyte Gulf, the St. Louis took two hits from Japanese aircraft, one of which tore a huge hole in the deck killing sixteen men, and another hit at about the water line on the forward port side. Neil Lombardi's battle station was as a loader on a 20 mm. anti-aircraft gun:

"The stress and concentration involved in the job overrode, to some extent, the feelings of intense fear. Also, there was a lot of adrenaline and the strange feeling of 'Is this really me? Is this really happening?' But I must say that there is something about looking at a kamikaze eyeball to eyeball which gives one a different perspective on things." *Some Reminiscences of World War Two*, supra, pp.21-22.

CHAPTER THIRTEEN

Perils of War

EARL STARK'S LST 572 returned to the East Coast of the United States from France. The October crossing was rough but his Naval Reserve captain was up to the challenge:

"During the return trip we encountered a severe hurricane and at one stage waves were breaking over our 75 foot high mast. One engine was at full speed ahead, the other at full speed reverse, in an attempt to maintain steerageway. To get caught in a trough could have been disastrous for this flat-bottomed war machine equipped with 50-caliber and 40-milimeter guns. It appeared our skipper had received adequate seamanship training.

"During the repair period that followed on the East Coast, one of our crew — a radioman — was taken off the ship. His name was William Pukall, the pronunciation of his last name being consistent with one who suffered from chronic seasickness." Earl R. Stark.

In November, the LST's skipper married a young lady from Roanoke:

"He brought her aboard on one occasion when we were anchored in the harbor. As she was climbing the Jacob's ladder, the Captain realized the skirt worn by his new bride was too revealing to the small boat crew below so he ordered 'eyes right.' Members of the small boat crew claim to this day (at least one is still alive) that the order was never heard." Earl Stark.

After extensive repairs, the 572 departed for the Pacific Theatre, to serve for the remainder of the war and for part of the Japanese occupation.

* * * * *

The "Heaven Can Wait" crew led a charmed life. The only crewman to earn a Purple Heart sustained his injury (minor) from a German buzz bomb that struck his hotel while he was on leave in London. All of the crew except Henry Bloch were Roman Catholics, who prayed before every mission. "I felt like I was getting a free ride." Henry Bloch.

The navigator's work station was immediately behind the bombardier's position in the nose of the B-17 aircraft. On one mission, Bloch went forward to watch a bomb drop and returned to find his seat blown out of the plane by enemy fire.

* * * * *

On November 30, 1944, twenty-two-year-old Fred Olander Jr., now with the Eighth Air Force's 379th Bomb Group, 527th Bomb Squadron, was shot down over Leipzig, Germany. It was his 28th mission ... at that time a tour of duty was 35 missions, followed by rotation back to the States.

The targets were refineries near Leipzig, and next to Berlin they were Germany's best defended locations. Forty bombers failed to return from this mission.

Fred described what happened to his plane, the squadron's lead ship:

"During this bomb run I earned my Purple Heart when a piece of shrapnel went through my helmet, grazing my forehead with enough authority to knock me out once we navigators had found the I.P. On the bomb run the bombardier navigates the plane so I really wasn't needed at the moment anyway. The anti-aircraft flak had hit more than me during the run and the plane was disabled, losing all oil. I came to very shortly before the pilot determined we should abandon ship. (The guys in the nose were putting my parachute on me when I revived.)

"We bailed out at about 5000 feet and all were captured. Leaving the plane was one of the noisiest times, with motors roaring and wind swishing. But as soon as the parachute opened I experienced the quietest time … there was no sound. The verbal parachute training we had slept through so many times came to reality and worked. My landing was with bent knees and rolling, as instructed. I was in a field and soon approached by Hitler Youth, swastika arm bands and all, saying something like 'pistola', and I stood with hands up.

"I was just outside the town of Heligenstadt and these kids collected my parachute and directed me into town. Two items remembered: a guy came in with my flight helmet and threw it at me, and I knew he didn't like us; the other … I started to wash my wound with some water I saw, and a lady stopped me, indicating it wasn't clean. She let me know that one of her family was a prisoner in the U.S. and was being well treated. Somehow, somewhere, I was turned over to the German military and taken by train to Frankfurt-on-Main, which was the interrogation center for all Air Force POWs."

Lieutenant Olander was imprisoned at Stalag Luft One, where Dave Smart was also a POW. But the camp held several thousand prisoners and he never encountered Dave.

Fred Olander Sr. learned on December 16 that his son had not returned from the November 30 mission, and an agonizing month passed before, on January 16, 1945, a telegram advised that Fred Jr. was a POW. A World War II telegram usually meant the worst — this one brought joy.

* * * * *

Ensign John Wells was assigned to a new destroyer escort, the Douglas A. Munro, and on December 7, 1944, the DE departed Norfolk, Virginia for the Pacific. The ship would escort convoys, patrol against submarines, and provide fire support for naval and amphibious operations at various island locations.

Also in December, after several months on Saipan, Bob Hanger's artillery battery staged the Great Saipan Beerbust — "a deliberate effort to let the enlisted guys blow off some steam while the officers and top NCOs drove the trucks, opened the beer, cooked the steaks and got dumped in the ocean." Robert C. Hanger. The conclusion of the event is described in *Who's gonna live*, supra, as follows:

"By about 1700 hours it had become obvious that the party was over. The beer and food were gone, all the officers and staff NCOs had been thrown in the ocean, and more and more of the celebrants were becoming immobile. It was about this time, too, that we realized that we had left camp without taking a roll call of the participants. That settled it. We scoured the area, loaded up and took off. Amazingly enough, we didn't lose anybody …" Page 45.

It was a highly successful effort to boost battery morale.

Wally Burger finally caught up with the Birmingham in San Francisco, where he was told that his arrival was long overdue. His duty aboard the Birmingham began in December 1944.

Nature could surpass warring mankind, and on December 18 our big chart in flag plot traced the course of a giant typhoon in the Philippine Sea. Despite warnings, three destroyers capsized, six other ships were heavily damaged, and 800 officers and men were lost. Admiral Nimitz pronounced it one of the Navy's greatest catastrophes.

* * * * *

Gordon Robertson returned to the Pacific Theater, where he was assigned duty on Oahu at Barber's Point Naval Air Station. Now an old hand with extensive combat experience, he instructed neophyte pilots in the tactics and missions that would be theirs upon joining a fleet squadron.

After thirty-one grueling bombing missions, Henry Bloch was rotated back to the United States. He had often felt cold sweat running down his back over Germany as deadly white antiaircraft puffs blossomed around the "Heaven Can Wait." Now he was safely ensconced in the Air Corps' Statistical Control School at Harvard University.

On New Year's Day, 1945, Ensign Wells saw for the first time the destruction that a kamikaze attack could inflict. The Munro was newly arrived at Espiritu Santo in the South Pacific. It had been a typically rough voyage for a DE crew, with seasickness rampant, and one of their first sights on entering the harbor was a destroyer with its entire superstructure blown off by a Japanese suicide plane.

Also in January, the Luce successfully withstood kamikaze attacks in Lingayen Gulf:

"That was the start of the Luce being called 'the Lucky Luce' from the survival of the morning and evening attacks." *DD 522: Diary of a Destroyer*, Ron Surels, 1994, Valley Graphics, Inc., Plymouth, N.H., p.79.

Cliff Jones was in Hawaii. He had been detached from the Luce to attend gunnery school in Honolulu, a pleasant assignment that lasted until March when he rejoined his ship.

Max Berry wrote Josephine on January 28:

"I have to clean my 2 guns every night. I have fired neither one of them except in practice since I got them, and I now have a tilted pelvis from that .45 automatic Colt." *One Man's WW II*, supra, p.200.

* * * * *

The Army's 1st Cavalry Division was delivered by the Navy to Lingayen Gulf on January 27, several days after the initial landing. A "flying squadron" of the 8th Cavalry Regiment was formed and ordered to move directly to Manila ahead of the other combat forces, to rescue the prisoners in the Santo Tomas prison. Jim Kemper's mechanized platoon was part of the squadron and ordered to defend a principal intersection of the Manila highway.

The Cavalry's troopers moved forward in the direction of the town of Cabanatuan.

The following day, soldiers from the elite U.S. Army 6th Ranger Battalion slipped behind enemy lines to rescue several hundred American and British POWs who had spent three hellish years in a camp near Cabanatuan. The Japanese Army was executing American prisoners in the Philippines as it retreated from the advancing US forces, and the American Army was headed that way. The Rangers freed the camp's prisoners before they could be killed. The story of their daring raid is told in *Ghost Soldiers*, by Hampton Sides (Doubleday, 2001).

Reaching Cabanatuan, the flying squadron prepared to race on to Manila as soon as General MacArthur gave the word. That word came, as described in *The Liberation of the Philippines, Volume XIII, History of United States Naval Operations in World War II*, by Samuel Eliot Morison, 1959, Little, Brown and Company:

"... The troopers were given additional stimulus by a personal message from General MacArthur ...:

'Go to Manila. Go around the Nips, bounce off the Nips, but go to Manila. Free the internees at Santo Tomas. Take Malacanan Palace and the Legislative Building.'" (pp.193-4).

The highway intersection defended by Jim Kemper's platoon became known as "Hot Corners" because of the amount of fighting there.

The platoon arrived at the intersection late in the day and hurriedly placed 37-millimeter anti-tank guns and armored personnel carriers to defend their position. That night a truckload of Japanese soldiers crashed into one of the personnel carriers and a platoon sergeant shot up the truck with a 50-caliber machine gun. Shortly afterward, Kemper heard one of the 37-millimeter tank guns firing:

"I ran down the road to this gun and found a complete squad of Japanese soldiers lying dead in the road before the gun, having been dropped by canister shot. Within a minute or two, as I stood by our gun, a small column of jeeps came down the road where the Japanese had come from and, lo and behold, there was General MacArthur in the second jeep, looking immaculate; very much the Supreme Commander. So I gave him a salute from the gun position as he passed by the bodies of the Japanese stretched out in a line along the road where he was driving. I was impressed that he was there at that time in a position of great danger, as the main body of the troops had not yet arrived at our position." James M. Kemper Jr.

Kemper and his platoon joined in the drive to Manila and upon arrival were assigned a position in one of the city blocks.

"That night, the second night of the flying squadron's arrival, there were explosions all over the city as the Japanese, having previously placed explosives at the bases of the principal buildings in Manila, blew up the most important structures in the city." James M. Kemper Jr.

Jim Kemper was wounded in Manila's street fighting, earning him a Purple Heart and additional points toward his Army discharge. After the war, Jim returned to Yale, graduating in March 1946. He became chairman and CEO of Commerce Bancshares, one of the mid-west's largest banking institutions.

* * * * *

The 39th Evacuation Hospital crossed the Rhine River and entered Germany. Their first night on German soil their quarters were rocked by an intense barrage — 25-inch shells fired from cannon on railroad tracks twenty-five miles away. The barrage was repeated the next night. The medical group returned to France ... the shelling was from the Battle of the Bulge in the Belgian woods, and the Hospital relocated to receive casualties.

During the Battle, Russell D. Shelden was in Liege, Belgium — the objective of a German army only eighteen miles away and the target of German V-1 buzz bombs. Commissioned a field artillery second lieutenant following graduation from the University of Missouri, Russ resigned his commission while in medical school and spent two years in the European Theater of Operations as a medical laboratory technician. He was now part of a 1000-bed General Hospital awaiting the Battle's end before setting up operations. Meanwhile, conditions for the American forces were desperate and, although a non-combatant medical soldier, Russ was issued a rifle and posted as guard of the Hospital's medical supply depot. The German advance was brought to a halt before it reached Russ, however.

The Hospital's proximity to the fighting continued throughout the war, and Russ Shelden earned three battle stars before VE Day. He then returned to medical school followed by a flourishing medical practice in anesthesiology, in Kansas City.

After the Battle, Dave Robinson and his medical colleagues moved back to Germany and an unforgettable experience:

"One day, about three weeks after the Battle of the Bulge, the officers and nurses were asked to proceed at once to trucks. We drove for about an hour and then the convoy stopped. We were ordered out of the trucks and were marched to a barracks-like building.

"We were absolutely shaken by the nauseating smells coming from the building. As we walked down its aisles we had to step over men, some dead, some living or trying to live under ghastly conditions. All of the men, living or dead, were so emaciated that they hardly had any power of movement. They suffered from vomiting, diarrhea, bloody stools, mucous from ruptured lungs, and pulmonary hemorrhages from tuberculosis and malnutrition. This was the concentration camp Buchenwald.

"The odors of the dead permeated the whole atmosphere.

"We were not brought to Buchenwald to treat these people. We were just to see them. The sights and smells of these bodies made the most ghastly dream a pleasure sequence instead."

David Robinson.

* * * * *

In India, Bill Deramus, now a major, carried a first class pass entitling him to railway transportation over the entire B & A Railway System ... penalty for loss of the pass, four rupees.

The trains were powered by coal:

"We had all coal burners and we had two firemen on 'em. Two native firemen. One of 'em was puttin' the coal down so the other could get it. And everything was done with a basket, a little basket. Used to fuel the engine that way ... It was something to watch 'em try to fill that tender ... they had never seen a scoop shovel." *Missouri Business*, November\December 1979, p.11.

And it was hot:

"The temperature would get up to 130 degrees with a hundred percent humidity. The first year I laughed at taking siestas in the afternoon from about 1 to 5. The second year I didn't laugh anymore."

Also there were local customs to be observed:

"They've got another strange rule over there. If you deposited a dead body on the station premises, it was up to the railroad to see it was buried."

CHAPTER FOURTEEN

Advanced Fleet Headquarters

CONGRESS PASSED A BILL establishing a new rank — Admiral of the Fleet — and Chester Nimitz became a five-star admiral.

The admiral visited Guam in the Mariana Islands, to determine its suitability for his advanced fleet headquarters. An American possession that fell to the Japanese in 1941, Guam was recaptured shortly before the Nimitz visit.

In January 1945, Nimitz began to transfer elements of the Cincpac planning and operations staff to Guam, moving closer to the action and leaving the war's administrative details behind for others to manage.

On January 7, I boarded the attack transport USS Drew and set out for the Marianas, 3800 miles west of Pearl Harbor. Special security precautions were imposed. The Drew's hold contained cargo which, though never identified or discussed, warranted the constant protection of a Marine guard. From the ship's bow we watched an escorting destroyer zig-zagging ahead of the Drew, on the alert for Japanese submarines.

The trip to Guam was uneventful, enlivened only by induction into the "silent mysteries of the Far East" when we reached the 180th meridian, the international dateline.

The indolent life of a passenger and the bland Navy chow combined to produce "irregularity." I finally consulted an indifferent pharmacist's mate. His medical advice: "Keep on eating ... you'll shit or bust."

The vast Pacific Ocean seemed to go on and on, a reminder that three-fourths of the world is covered by water. The trip required ten days. Even after we arrived at our destination there remained a long stretch of ocean separating us from the Chinese mainland. And we were more than 1500 miles from Tokyo, our ultimate objective.

On January 19, the Drew dropped anchor in Guam's Apra Harbor. We made the jolting trip up to our new hilltop headquarters sitting on a truckload of classified cargo from the ship. En route we dodged falling rocks which the Navy's Seabees were blasting out of a cliff near the harbor, a rude introduction to the Forward Area. At home there would have been warning signs and men with red flags. The Seabees on Guam expected military traffic to look out for itself.

A February press release disclosed Cincpac's new location on Guam. My duties at the advanced headquarters were no different than they had been at Pearl Harbor, although here Cincpac was housed in a modest frame building instead of the elaborate bomb-proof fortress that had sheltered us back in Hawaii.

We arrived near the end of dry season, to find tropical Guam warm and dusty. Neckties were discarded and shorts were acceptable. Drinking water was tepid, stored in lister bags — canvas contraptions hung from tripods in the shade and "cooled" by condensation. After 1700 hours, cold beer was available in a small quonset hut officers' club christened "The Coconut Log."

The dinner menu often included greenish Australian mutton. M & M candy withstood well the rigors of travel and climate, and satisfied a sweet tooth. Weevils found their way into the flour, and the Navy cooks simply baked them into the bread. Reluctant diners, with a bow to Madison Avenue, christened the fortified product "weevil bread."

* * * * *

Seabees constructed two-story quonset huts with concrete floors to serve as B.O.Q.s. There was no air-conditioning but Cincpac's hilltop location was cooler at night than the rest of the island.

Guam's capital city of Agana was a shambles, most of its Chamorro residents homeless. American naval guns and artillery had reduced their houses to heaps of rubble. But the incomparable Seabees were at work restoring Agana and the remainder of the island. Villages sprang up overnight, neat and substantial.

The Chamorros of Guam, Navy stewards' mates for generations, were fiercely loyal to the United States — a country that most of them had never seen. Guam had been wrested from Spain in 1898 by the Spanish-American War, a conflict that marked the birth of the United States as a world power. Now, they welcomed the Americans' recapture of their island and cheered the American guns even as their homes were being pulverized by them.

* * * * *

The Marianas quickly became bases for fleets of giant B-29 bombers of the 21st Bomber Command. Their first raid on Japan occurred January 19, 1945, the day of my arrival. These were massive air strikes, a far cry from Jimmy Doolittle's defiant Hornet-based B-25 attack on Tokyo in April of 1942. Nightly the "superforts" roared aloft from fields on Guam, Saipan and Tinian, and flew the long air route to the Japanese home islands. It was an exhausting 14-hour trip, over the open Pacific except for the brief, frightful ordeal of enemy fire in the skies over Japan.

I visited the bombers' Northwest field on Guam, where mechanics swarmed over returned aircraft, repairing damage from flak and bullets, checking and double-checking for airworthiness. Despite their care, there were occasional disasters. Some nights, I saw a column of fire leap upward from the airfield — the funeral pyre of a B-29 crew whose heavily-laden plane with its 20,000 pound bomb load had failed to clear the ground. The bomber crews that came after them had to fly through the smoke and flame, praying that their own planes would survive takeoff.

There were rumors of a standing invitation to replace Army Air Corps gunners and see Tokyo by B-29, but there were no takers.

54

CHAPTER FIFTEEN

Life on Guam; and a President Dies

GUAM OFFERED MORE EXCITEMENT than Pearl Harbor. Long after our advance base was established, Japanese stragglers remained at large on the island, continuing to snipe and ambush. Occasionally, lone Japanese were sighted stealthily watching American movies from the edge of the jungle. Meanwhile patrols of Chamorro police combed the forests and mountains, hunting down fugitives.

Units with loudspeakers broadcast news of American victories and invited surrender, with little success. An occasional Japanese gave himself up, but this was rare; as on Manus, the Japanese soldier on Guam fought to the death or took his own life when cornered rather than dishonor his ancestors. American Marines found the suicidal bias of the Japanese fighting man incomprehensible but accommodated him.

Marine sentries were under orders to shoot anything that moved at night without a light, and occasionally they did — once with tragic results when a Seabee guard was killed. Consequently we always brandished a lighted flashlight when going to and from a midwatch.

Although reports of skulking Japanese ceased, truck wheels were still blown off by land mines and grisly reminders of battle — bones and skulls, the smell of decaying bodies, bits of clothing and belts of ammunition — permeated the island. There were no more snipers or banzai suicide charges, but Guam was never entirely at peace until the end of the war.

* * * * *

Meanwhile, khaki-clad war correspondents descended on Guam by the hundreds. The unfettered flow of information was an early casualty of the war and, like our letters home, their dispatches were censored to protect military secrets.

The correspondents were usually quartered in the Cincpac area. As the war moved on, they departed for other battlegrounds or to cover engagements from shipboard, some returning between campaigns.

One correspondent who found his way to Cincpac hill was Alvin S. McCoy, dispatched to the Pacific by the *Kansas City Star* to write about personnel from the Kansas City area. McCoy wrote a piece about "The City of Kansas City," a B-29 based on Guam that participated in fire-bomb raids on Japanese cities. The incendiary plane had another, more apropos name: "The Firebug."

* * * * *

USO tours stopped in the Marianas, bringing music and laughter and pretty girls. Lovely starlets who could dance or sing were enthusiastically received. The most applauded programs were those of the big bands of Dick Jergens and the Navy's own Claude Thornhill. The performers brought reminders of home and were much appreciated by the armed forces.

The war's staple diversion, the motion picture, rescued us from boredom ... tedium relieved by reels of celluloid. The theatres were spartan — the deck of a ship or a jungle clearing — but moving pictures were never enjoyed more. Blonde Betty Grable and red-haired Rita Hayworth came to life in technicolor on the screen, and for a little time the war was far away.

* * * * *

One day my duties took me to the remote headquarters of the Forward Area Command, on neighboring Saipan — a Japanese island until captured a few months earlier. While there I spoke to a lanky lieutenant commander, briefly interrupting his reading of an old issue of "Time" magazine. He looked vaguely familiar. Then I recognized him — Henry Fonda, an actor whose movies I had enjoyed before the war and who would later draw upon Navy experience in his portrayal of "Mr. Roberts" in the hit play of that name.

Commander Fonda had told the press: "I don't want to sell war bonds or be photographed with soldiers and sailors. I want to be a sailor."

* * * * *

We waited with curiosity for the rains to begin. When the monsoons arrived, daytime cloudbursts brought sheets of rain. At night the rain drummed fortissimo on the corrugated metal roof of the B.O.Q. It often seemed to rain horizontally on Guam, when water blew into our sleeping quarters and soaked our beds despite wide slanting eaves jutting far beyond the second-story windows.

Heat and humidity produced prickly heat ..."jungle crud" that afflicted many.

Mildew was everywhere. Clothes became moldy. I replaced my disintegrating leather wristwatch strap with a canvas band. The Navy issued "souwesters" — rain gear reminiscent of the old sailing days of wooden ships and iron men. And our heavy, high-topped "boondocker" shoes splattered the sloppy red mud underfoot. Officers thirsty for a cold beer stood soddenly in the warm rain outside the Coconut Log … it was too small to shelter more than a handful of patrons.

* * * * *

I saw Admiral Nimitz occasionally. With his white hair and dignified bearing he presented a distinguished appearance, and a calm confidence befitting his rank and role. A Texan, he was as tough as rawhide underneath a placid, blue-eyed exterior, undaunted by the awful responsibility resting in his hands. He enjoyed the respect and admiration of the flag staff, and cheerfully complied with requests for his endorsement on paper money … the "short snorters" collected by World War II servicemen. Chester W. Nimitz was "as respected and revered as any senior officer in World War II." *The Navy,* Navy Historical Foundation, 2000, published by Hugh Lauter Levin Associates, Inc., page 141.

Vice Admiral Charles H. McMorris was second-in-command at Cincpac. His peers had long ago dubbed him "Soc" — after the Greek sage Socrates. Soc's intellect was much prized by his colleagues. And, a good exec, he insulated Nimitz from much detail. As Edwin P. Hoyt notes in *How They Won the War in the Pacific* (Weybright and Talley, New York, 1970):

> "... his quick yeses and quicker nos were famous in the fleet." (page 467)

McMorris worked long hours, carried a heavy load, and was much admired by his Cincpac juniors.

There was a command struggle between Admiral Nimitz and General Douglas MacArthur. MacArthur we regarded as something of an egomaniac, with a genius for publicizing his own triumphs.

56

December 7, 1941
USS Shaw explodes
at Pearl Harbor
(EPH)

1941-1942 University of Missouri Basketball Team
Earl R. Stark — rear, second from left
Author front right
"Missouri Basketball Players on Western Tour"
(Kansas City Star, December 1941)

The bombing of Pearl Harbor
did not prevent the trip.

Daily Navy calisthenics
M.U. parade ground
1943 Savitar
(M.U. Yearbook)

M.U. ROTC
field artillery battery
1943 Savitar

Reserve Office Training was compulsory for freshman and sophomore men.

Chief Petty Officer and All-American quarterback,
Paul Christman
1943 Savitar

Later a professional football star and TV sports commentator, Christman was assigned by the Navy to a diesel engine training school at MU.

Fordham 2, Missouri 0
Kansas City's Don Greenwood is the punter.

1942 Sugar Bowl game
1942 Savitar

Zealous wartime censors prevented Sugar Bowl sportscasters from disclosing the monsoon weather.

Stephens College girls entertain in their ballroom and lounge.
1943 Savitar

Upper right: A Christian College girl and her convoy set out.
Lower: Sailors mixing with University coeds in front of Journalism School archway.
1943 Savitar

Scrap metal pile outside Delta Upsilon Fraternity House. Students collected scrap metal for the Junk Dealers' Ball.
1943 Savitar

"Don't just stand there — go get the new catalog!"
Drawing by Jack B. O'Hara

Jack B. O'Hara, a talented artist, was commissioned a second lieutenant in the Army's Medical Administrative Corps. An early assignment was the Kansas City Medical Depot.

Polo player Jack R. Ridge inspects Military Dept. horses
1943 Savitar

The horses that pulled the ROTC field artillery batteries doubled as mounts for the MU polo team.

Gordon Robertson's plane is retrieved from Narragansett Bay after a night-time training flight mishap.

Photo courtesy of Gordon H. Robertson

Cliff Jones aboard the "Lucky Luce."
The Luce's luck ran out off Okinawa.
Photo courtesy of Cliff Jones

George Tourtellot and Aleutian friends. Lieutenant Tourtellot, a radar expert and ultimate casualty, set up radar stations in the Aleutian Islands.
Photo courtesy of Sally Tourtellot Ruddy

"Rosie the Riveter" and "Wanda the Welder" labored in Kansas City's Pratt & Whitney aircraft engine plant, and for 63 cents an hour built B-25 "Billy Mitchell" medium bombers at the North American Aviation plant where half the employees were women.

Rosie the Riveter at work

All photos by Wilborn & Associates, Photographers

Mothers supported their sons and daughters in the service in many ways and proudly wore pins with blue stars to honor them.

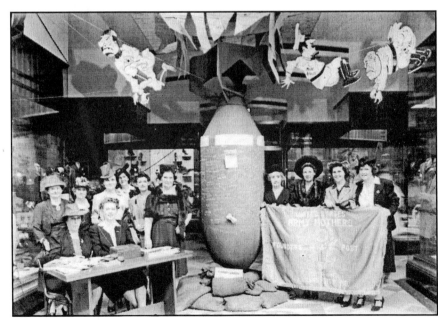

Paper drive by neighborhood patriots —
The kids pitched in.
Wilborn & Associates, Photographers

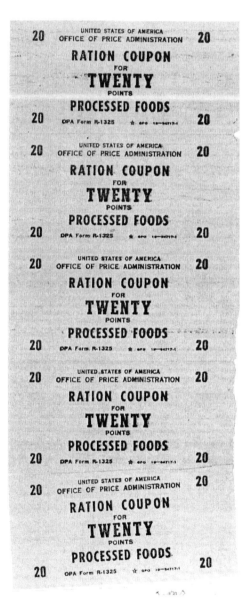

OPA-rationed food was supplemented
by Victory Gardens' produce

Darby built and launched landing craft for the beaches
of Europe, Africa and the Pacific
Wilborn & Associates, Photographers

CLASS OF SERVICE
This is a full-rate
Telegram or Cable-
gram unless its de-
ferred character is in-
dicated by a suitable
symbol above or pre-
ceding the address.

WESTERN UNION

1201

SYMBOLS
DL = Day Letter
NL = Night Letter
LC = Deferred Cable
NLT = Cable Night Letter
Ship Radiogram

A. N. WILLIAMS   NEWCOMB CARLTON   J. C. WILLEVER
PRESIDENT   CHAIRMAN OF THE BOARD   FIRST VICE-PRESIDENT

The filing time shown in the date line on telegrams and day letters is STANDARD TIME at point of origin. Time of receipt is STANDARD TIME at point of destination.

1351 51/50 NL=COLUMBIA MO 16

EDWARD T MATHENY=

7121 PENN KSC=   Duplicate of Telegram

PURSUANT OF REQUEST FROM NAVY THAT UNIVERSITY FACILITATE
YOUR INDUCTION INTO V-7 AM NOW INFORMING YOU AND NAVY
THAT I WILL RECOMMEND TO FACULTY YOU BE RECOMMENDED FOR
GRADUATION WITHOUT MEETING MINOR REQUIREMENTS NOT YET
FULFILLED IF YOU THUS ENTER SERVICE THERE IS EVERY
PRESUMPTION FACULTY WILL APPROVE MY RECOMMENDATION=

    W C CURTIS DEAN.

V-7.   THE COMPANY WILL APPRECIATE SUGGESTIONS FROM ITS PATRONS CONCERNING ITS SERVICE

The MU faculty authorized the author's early graduation.

Midshipman School at
Camp MacDonough,
Plattsburg, New York,
followed MU graduation

Base entrance of frigid
Camp MacDonough in winter,
twenty miles south of
Canadian border (USNT)

Midshipmen marching
to class.
Spring came at last.
(USNT)

Commando Run at
Camp MacDonough.
Physical fitness was stressed.
(USNT)

The whaleboat coxswain's puzzling command: "Stand by to give way together."

Small boat seamanship instruction on Lake Champlain. Most of the class were destined for amphibious craft.
(USNT)

Midshipmen ignored the athletic specialist's urging to "Punish yourselves, men," but the camp boxing tournament was required of all. (USNT)

The Midshipman band's weekly radio program
was named "Hats Off to the Navy."
(USNT)

A few members of Company K. Author back row, left end.
We were together in our resolve to win the war.

Gunnery instruction; amphibious craft mounted nothing this large.

The chapel, where we sang the Navy hymn:
"Hear us when we cry to thee for those in peril on the sea."

Bing Crosby greets Dr. Robinson (far right) and colleagues.

Litter carriers taking a patient
from receiving to the ward.
39th Evactuation Hospital at work

All photos courtesy of David Robinson, M.D.

David Robinson (right) and colleague
Columbia Presbyterian Hospital, New York, N.Y.

The 39th Evacuation Hospital tent
The hospital and Dr. Robinson
earned five combat ribbons.

Colorado photos from
USS Colorado Cruise Book
1942-1946
Courtesy of
William H. Woodson

Camouflage-painted USS
Colorado (carriers in distance)

USS MacKenzie puts to sea.
Photo courtesy of
Albert C. Bean Jr.

Colorado crewmen dive in,
while small boat stands by as
a precaution.

Lt. Henry W. Bloch, Navigator
Eighth Air Force
He flew 31 grueling bombing missions in
his B-17, the "Heaven Can Wait."
Photo courtesy of Henry W. Bloch

The above photograph of David Douglas Duncan on
Bougainville in the Solomon Islands was taken by a
young Navy lieutenant, Richard M. Nixon — later
President of the United States.

Flying Fortress (B-17)
Wilborn & Associates, Photographers

Service men at a Kansas City Union Station information booth were directed to the Service Men's Club and its amenities.

War bonds were sold at the union station.
Quotas for war bond sales were regularly exceeded.

All photos by Wilborn & Associates, Photographers

USO canteens were popular, operated by hospitable volunteers.

Conway Leary's P-51 was shot down while strafing German aircraft. He finished the war as a POW.
Photo courtesy of Conway Leary

Edward T. Matheny Sr., a proud ex-marine, with the author on the eve of departure for Hawaii

General Douglas MacArthur and Admiral Chester Nimitz They put aside their command differences to defeat the Japanese.   (EPH)

Sally Tourtellot and Bette Lou Giboney sold defense stamps in Kansas City's Union Station.
(Photo courtesty of Sally Tourtellot-Ruddy)

He presented a constant challenge to the Navy public relations specialists, who believed that the Navy and the Marine Corps should share with him in the credit for the successful prosecution of the war in the Pacific.

* * * * *

The death of President Roosevelt occurred on April 12, 1945, and at 7:09 p.m. that evening Harry S Truman became president of the United States.

Roosevelt had been in ill health for many months, but the gravity of his illness was not generally known. He had been elected to an unprecedented fourth term the previous November. I was just nine years old when he first became president, and it seemed to me that he had occupied the White House forever ... a perception that I shared with my contemporaries in the armed forces. To us he had been the embodiment of the Presidency.

David Duncan was also on Guam at this time:

"Here, as everywhere I'm sure, the death of President Roosevelt came as a chilling jolt. Who knows what he was carrying in his head! His personal contact with Churchill. His extraordinary image of leadership in times of crisis. That voice which put shape to dreams, and dreams to lofty purpose." Page 153. *Yankee Nomad,* supra.

FDR's failing health had little effect on the conduct of the war, however. And upon his death, although at Cincpac headquarters we mourned our country's loss at special memorial services, it was business as usual.

* * * * *

There was great curiosity concerning Harry S Truman, FDR's successor in the White House. As a Kansas Citian, I was expected by my comrades to be an authority on our new president from neighboring Independence. The *Kansas City Star,* a Republican newspaper, often lambasted Truman, former political ally of Democratic boss Thomas J. Pendergast, and I harbored reservations about his presidential qualifications. To me at the time, his inauguration proved that anyone could become president of the United States.

Truman's reaction to Roosevelt's death, when he was thrust into the presidency after only eighty-two days as vice president, was not reassuring:

"When they told me yesterday what had happened, I felt like the moon, the stars and all the planets had fallen on me."

But misgivings were soon forgotten as the war effort went forward without missing a beat.

* * * * *

On Easter Sunday, 1945, church services were held in the mess hall that served as the Cincpac chapel. The highlight was a four-minute "blue network" radio broadcast to the United States. I wondered if my family back home was listening. World War II coined the phrase "There are no atheists in foxholes," and religion fortified fighting men. Chaplains of all faiths were important to the armed forces; they were comforting whatever might be their religious persuasion — all of them enjoyed an inside track with God, and could put in a good word for us.

* * * * *

David Kemper was injured in a jeep accident, but on April 16, 1945, wrote his brother Jim: "My knee is about well and I am about to join the festivities again up North." David was no longer with a headquarters company but was with C Troop of the 81st Cavalry. And on April 25, just two weeks before VE Day, David Woods Kemper was killed by enemy action in Italy's Po Valley, while engaged in dangerous reconnaissance work. The news of his brother's death had a profound effect on Jim Kemper:

"His death changed my life very abruptly and was a very sobering experience at the age of twenty-four. I will always remember my brother as he was then — twenty-six years old, handsome, full of grit and full of fun."

The beautiful fountain at Eighth and Main in Kansas City, Missouri is David Woods Kemper's memorial, commissioned by his family.

CHAPTER SIXTEEN

Victory in Europe; the Pacific War goes on

THE WAR IN EUROPE ENDED with V E Day on May 9, 1945. Fred Olander Jr. learned of this when the disappearance of his German prison camp guards was followed a few hours later by the arrival of Russian troops:

"We went to bed one night and the next morning found that we no longer had guards, That afternoon in marched part of the Russian army driving confiscated cows ahead of them and that night we had beef and their USO troop putting on a show for us. One point I will always remember is their insistence that each of us start wearing a black arm band out of respect for our deceased President Roosevelt. We were detained by the Russians for about one week while they cleared all of our names through their system and then we were flown out by the 8th Air Force to LeHavre." Fred Olander.

Lieutenant Olander's war was effectively at an end. He would return to civilian life with the Air Medal and three oak leaf clusters, the Purple Heart, and other decorations.

As for others in the European theatre:

"All anyone cared about now was getting home. The war was won and the only fear that lurked in anyone's head was the Pacific. They wouldn't send us there for an invasion of Japan, would they? It didn't seem like our war over there." *My War,* supra.

Redman Callaway's truck company was in Le Havre, France, when news of the German surrender "flashed across Europe." Red's celebration was tempered by the continuing war in the Pacific and "the constant rumors that some units were already being shipped to the States for reassignment to the Far East ... our future rode on the gossip that circulated all summer long." *White Captain *** Black Troops,* supra, pages 120-121.

Now a personnel officer at a B-29 base near Hays, Kansas, Henry Bloch was discharged and returned to civilian life, also with the Air Medal and three oak leaf clusters, as well as other decorations.

On VE Day, German U-boats were instructed to surface and report their positions. Two of them surfaced west of the Straits of Gibraltar where the MacKenzie was patrolling. The MacKenzie escorted its former quarry to Gibraltar where the British accepted their surrender. Then, its months of shore bombardment, blockades and convoy duty in the Mediterranean at an end, the MacKenzie returned to the United States for overhaul and then departed to train in Cuba for duty in the Pacific. However, the war's end intervened:

"Fortunately, Japan's later surrender made the MacKenzie's services unnecessary."

Albert C. Bean Jr.

Japan's later surrender was welcome intervention for David Robinson also:

"The war continued in the Pacific. I was reassigned to a new evacuation hospital, assuming that I'd be going to the Pacific theater. This didn't happen. Thank goodness."

David Robinson.

Conway Leary, liberated by General Patton's troops on April 29, 1945, celebrated VE Day in Ingolstadt, Germany. The party was in the 13th century home of the town's burgomaster, with Glenn Miller records played on a hand-cranked Victrola, and champagne from a well-stocked wine cellar. The next day, Conway started the long trip home, returning to the United States on June 3. A telephone call to Kansas City from Boston informed him that he now had a son.

On VE Day, Herman Johnson was back in the United States. After some twenty months overseas, he had returned as the Executive Officer of Colonel (later General) Benjamin Davis Jr., the leader of the Tuskeegee Airmen now charged with command of a group training for combat in the Pacific Theater. The 447th Bomber/Fighter Group was scheduled for Okinawa when the atom bomb interrupted their travel plans. Herman Johnson later became a successful businessman and civic leader in Kansas City.

On May 13, Dave Smart flew to Rouen, France, and then sailed for home on a Coast Guard ship out of Le Havre. After sixty days' leave he was ordered to Miami, Florida, where he was when the war with Japan ended.

* * * * *

The end of the war in Europe was not a cause for jubilation in the Pacific Theater, where war continued unabated:

"7,8,9 May, 1945. The European war is over for practical purposes. But everyone here believes it won't do us a bit of good … The feeling is that the Japs will be so hard to root out at home that it will take twice the number of combat men and officers."

One Man's WW II, supra, p.230.

The Munro served in the assault and occupation of Borneo from May 19 to July 5, where mines around the small island of Tarakan posed a particular problem. An enemy battery devastated the minesweeping force for much of the month of May until the Munro took a hand:

"The most troublesome spot was a concealed enemy battery at Cape Djoeata, the high point on the northwestern side of Tarakan. On May 2, it suddenly opened up on the sweepers as they were working the narrow channel north and west of Tarakan. A hit caused the YMS-481 to explode and sink; two other YMS were hit but survived … This battery defied all efforts to eliminate it until 23 May, when the destroyer escort Douglas A. Munro gave it a thorough working over with 5-inch and automatic weapons, which knocked out the two 75-mm guns of which it consisted." *The Liberation of the Philippines*, supra, page 262.

* * * * *

The commander of the British Pacific Fleet called on Admiral Nimitz one day late in May to present him with knighthood in the Order of the Bath. With the end of the war in Europe, more British ships were now available to fight the Japanese. The increased presence of these staunch allies was reassuring.

The British officers wore immaculate white uniforms, many in short pants that did not detract one iota from their dignity and air of command. Newsreel cameras outside the Cincpac administration building recorded the occasion for the world to see.

Trucks carried the crews of the British ships, anchored in the harbor, about the island. And officers of the American Navy were occasionally invited aboard the British vessels. These invitations were prized. Our ships were "dry," whereas the hospitable British "spliced the main brace" with their American guests. One Cincpac officer reported that his host offered three toasts, ceremoniously opening a new bottle of scotch with each drink.

Meanwhile on Cincpac hill, the cramped Coconut Log was replaced by a more spacious dispensary. Mixed drinks were available, and cheap. When the Navy bartender commented on the popularity of his 10-cent martinis, he learned that the attraction was not their generous proportions or the bargain price — his customers were ordering them for the olives, otherwise unattainable.

In June, after completing 750 hours of flying the Hump including 108 combat missions, Tom Thompson was due for rotation back to the States. Still with the Air Transport Command in India, he awaited those orders.

* * * * *

I boarded one of our submarines, the Archer-fish, at the invitation of Gordon Crosby, a University of Missouri Sigma Chi from the small Ozark town of Eldon. After the war, Gordon became Chairman, President and CEO of U.S. Life Corporation. But now he was Ensign Crosby, the sub's communications officer.

The previous November off the shore of the island of Honshu, the Archer-fish put six torpedoes into the Japanese carrier Shinano, then the heaviest warship ever built at 70,000 tons. The Shinano was only seventeen hours into her maiden voyage and just sixty-five miles from Japan when she went to the bottom. The feat is the subject of the book *SHINANO! The Sinking of Japan's Super Warship* by her skipper, the late Captain Joseph F. Enright, U.S.N.

My visit below decks in this boat only 311 feet long and 27 feet wide was claustrophobic, even though the Archer-fish was moored peacefully in Guam's Apra Harbor. Today's nuclear submarines are spacious compared to the World War II subs.

* * * * *

From time to time, I encountered other acquaintances from home who saw action against the Japanese. I particularly recall an old friend, Marine Lieutenant Charles I. Campbell, who bravely fought his way ashore during the Marianas invasion, unscathed. When I saw him, his unit was in Hawaii preparing for another island assault — bloody Iwo Jima. Now a realistic combat veteran, Chuck recognized that he might not survive another such battle. "A veteran infantryman is a terrified infantryman" was the maxim and even greater bravery was required of veterans such as Chuck, although his emotion seemed to be more fatalism than fear. And Chuck was in fact seriously wounded on Iwo Jima where, according to Admiral Nimitz: " uncommon valor was a common virtue."

Recovering from his wounds, Chuck remained in the Marine Corps after the war, retiring as a lieutenant colonel following many years spent in loyal service to his country.

Almost all of my friends survived the war. That M.U. history professor's prediction had been accurate back in 1941: 328 University of Missouri students gave their lives in World War II. Meanwhile, morale was high. Most young men in the service — confident of victory and youthful immortality — managed to live for the day and not speculate unduly on what the morrow might bring.

* * * * *

After one and a half years of checking the teeth of B-29 crews in Pratt, Kansas, Grant Hatfield was sent to the Philippines. Following stops at Ulithi and Eniwetok, his ship arrived at Manila in July, 1945.

Two days later he flew to Zamboanga, on the island of Mindinao. And four days after that he contracted a case of hepatitis and was hospitalized for eight weeks.

After his release from the hospital, Dr. Hatfield attended to the dental needs of personnel at a nearby Army Air Corps base. He also made an effort to conform to his new environment, living very briefly in a small grass hut on the beach:

> "When I retired for the night I placed my shoes under my cot. My front and only door was a screen door. That night the tide came into my chambers and my shoes floated out to sea. I moved the next day." Grant Hatfield.

While on Zamboanga, Grant adopted a Rhesus monkey. A picture of a shirtless Grant and his pet disproved a lyric of the time that "the monkeys have no tails on Zamboanga."

A Christmas greeting was further evidence to his mother that Dr. Hatfield had "gone native." After Grant was invited by a school teacher for lunch in a village, he posed with his hostess for a photograph surrounded by village children. Later, Grant mailed home copies of the photograph, wishing family and friends a "Merry Christmas from the Hatfields of Zamboanga."

Jack O'Hara was also sent to the Philippines, landing at Tacloban. After a few weeks at the Leyte Replacement Depot, he was assigned to a Medical Depot on the outskirts of Manila. Later, believing that his artistic talent could be put to better use, he applied for and was assigned duty as an artist at H.Q. Base X in Manila, where he was employed designing posters for the prevention of venereal disease among the troops. He also found time to sketch one of Manila's ruined buildings.

CHAPTER SEVENTEEN

Fifth Fleet, the Atom Bomb and VJ Day

ON AUGUST 1, 1945, I reported to Fifth Fleet Commander Raymond A. Spruance for duty on his staff.

Lieutenant William Crickard, Admiral Spruance's senior plotting officer, had been offered reassignment to the West Coast if he could find a suitable replacement. His duties were similar to mine and, wanting sea duty, I volunteered for the transfer. However, my enthusiasm waned somewhat with Bill Crickard's farewell disclaimer: "If you get out there and get your ass blown off, don't blame me."

The Fifth Fleet staff were neighbors on Cincpac hill, and I moved my gear into their quonset hut B.O.Q. where Navy captains, Army and Marine colonels, and numerous lesser ranks all lived together in informal camaraderie. I enjoyed being a part of it. Everyone joined in the social events, organized by the "Fifth Fleet Chowder, Marching and Needlepoint Society."

I met with Admiral Spruance shortly after reporting for duty. Spruance had been the victor in the Battle of Midway — fought from June 2 to June 6, 1942, not ashore on tiny Midway Island as the name suggested but totally at sea. His Fifth Fleet ships and planes destroyed the carrier striking force of the Japanese navy. It was the most significant carrier battle in history, and is regarded by military historians as the turning point of the Pacific war. The admiral, a slender, soft-spoken man, shook hands with me, and asked if I were "looking for excitement." I answered with a guarded "Yes" and received his solemn assurance that I would find it with him. I recalled my predecessor's words about parting with my rear end.

* * * * *

The Fifth Fleet utilized the same warships as Admiral Halsey's Third Fleet. The flag staffs were different, however. By alternating commands it was possible, when one was at sea, for the other to be ashore planning the next campaign. "The team remains the same but the drivers change," explained Admiral Nimitz.

Spruance took over from Halsey on January 27, 1945: "He had a wonderful reputation to live up to, and he did." *The Liberation of the Philippines*, supra, page 183.

The Fifth Fleet staff was between operations when I joined it, plotting the invasion of the Japanese home islands. This terrible, final assault on Japan was to be a Fifth Fleet operation. It was apparent, as I began to learn something about "Operation Olympic," that tremendous losses on both sides were anticipated. The Allies expected a suicidal defense by the men and women, and even the children, of Japan. I better understood Admiral Spruance's allusion to "excitement." The admiral had little enthusiasm for the battles confronting his fleet, but the pressure for invasion mounted daily.

* * * * *

Meanwhile, the cruiser USS Indianapolis was sunk by a Japanese submarine with great loss of life. The Indianapolis alternated as the Fifth Fleet flagship, and the flag staff lost friends when she went to the bottom.

The "Indy" brought atomic bomb parts for assembly on the island of Tinian in the Marianas. She made the long voyage from California's Mare Island Navy base with the bombs' uranium 235 core welded to the deck in the admiral's cabin.

Skeptics questioned how the new weapon would perform. When Truman came to office in 1945, he inherited FDR's chief of staff … the brusque Admiral William D. Leahy. Leahy, present when his commander-in-chief first learned of the frightful weapon, predicted that the bomb would "never go off."

Shortwave radio broadcasts from Guam by a Japanese-speaking admiral, beamed to Japan every day at noon, had begun to warn of a new weapon of mass destruction. But on July 31, Japan rejected the Potsdam ultimatum — to accept unconditional surrender or face annihilation. And on August 6, at 8:15 a.m., the first atomic bomb was dropped on Hiroshima by the Enola Gay, a B-29 based on nearby Tinian. The bomb did indeed "go off," and 140,000 people died. President Truman, aboard the cruiser Augusta en route to Washington from his Potsdam meeting with Churchill and Stalin, declared:

"The force from which the sun draws its power has been loosed against those who brought war to the Far East."

Despite the "pika-don" (flash-bang), the Japanese stubbornly fought on, and the devastation of Hiroshima was followed on August 9 by a second A-bomb from another Marianas-based B-29. This one leveled much of Nagasaki and shocked Japan into surrender; on August 14, Japan accepted the Potsdam "unconditional surrender" demand. On August 15, Emperor Hirohito himself ordered an end to hostilities:

* * * * *

When the A-bomb was dropped on Hiroshima, an "eyes only" secret dispatch to Cincpac — intended for top brass alone — described a huge, mushroom-shaped cloud rising miles in the air over the city. Thus was cryptically conveyed to Lieutenant Robert Bergstrom, the Communication Watch Officer, the news that the age of atomic warfare had dawned. Following protocol, Bergstrom recruited Dan Dietrich, Cincpac Communications Officer, to read proof with him on the message. As he read, Dietrich could only ask: "What the hell is that?" But security about a terrible new weapon was not airtight. Stories circulated on Guam prior to August 6 of Army airmen betting that the war would be over in ten days.

A *Kansas City Times* banner headline on August 15, 1945, proclaimed "Japs Bow to Terms — Mac Arthur to Rule." The story began: "Japan surrendered unconditionally tonight. History's most destructive war is over except for formalities." However, according to another newspaper account, Bull Halsey was dubious:

"It looks like the war is over. Cease firing but if you see any enemy planes in the air shoot them down in friendly fashion."

* * * * *

Since that August many years ago there has been debate over the morality of President Truman's decision to use atomic bombs to end the war that, for America, began with Japan's sneak attack on Pearl Harbor. I have always regarded the Bomb as an instrument of deliverance and have never doubted that President Truman chose the correct, even humanitarian, course of action.

It has been argued that Japan was on the verge of capitulation in August, 1945, and the A-bombs were unnecessary. However, Emperor Hirohito's surrender order belies that:

"... the enemy has begun to use a new and most cruel bomb, the power of which to do damage is indeed incalculable, taking the toll of many innocent lives ... This is the reason why We have ordered the acceptance of the provisions of the Joint declaration of the Powers ...." *The Making of the Atomic Bomb*, Richard Rhodes, 1986, Simon & Schuster, Inc.

As is noted in Ronald H. Spector's *Eagle Against the Sun*, supra, none of the critics of Truman's atom bomb decisions could demonstrate that Japan would have surrendered without the use of two atomic bombs:

"The most careful and authoritative study of Japan's decision to surrender notes that 'although the atomic attack on Hiroshima made it impossible for anyone present to continue to deny the urgency of Japan's situation, it apparently had not made a deep enough impression on the chiefs of staff and the War Minister as to make them willing to cast their lot outright for a termination of the war.' Some of the Japanese leaders were already speculating that perhaps the Americans had but one bomb or that a defense could be quickly improvised." (page 559).

Enormous casualties would have resulted from an invasion of the Japanese home islands, casualties dwarfing D Day's toll. No one who expected to participate in that bloody Gotterdammerung experienced regret over the use of atomic bombs to end the war. Veteran American troops, spared the final confrontation with a Japanese military that knew no surrender and a civilian populace prepared to die for the Emperor with explosive-laden children trained to throw themselves beneath tank treads, wept with relief and joy. They were going to survive!

On the home front, there was no questioning of Truman's decision. "Thank God for Harry Truman" was the sentiment in Kansas City. *Over Here*, supra.

David Douglas Duncan, on Zamboanga when the surrender "scuttlebutt" came over the radio, wrote of the reaction to the news:

"Maybe you heard us — and all the other guys all over the whole wide Pacific. It *must* have been the same everyplace ... Should know within twenty-four hours what the future of the war will be. But if the atomic bombs that destroyed Hiroshima and Nagasaki are as frightful as claimed by those first announcements, then this war is now history ... And so are they." *Yankee Nomad*, supra, page 178.

The world's first nuclear explosion occurred in New Mexico on July 16, 1945, one day after my twenty-second birthday anniversary. Whether or not to use this new weapon of mass destruction was not an abstract, ethical question. The Bomb would mean that I — and a million like me — would live to celebrate other anniversaries.

The December 7, 1997 issue of *The Boston Globe* published an article by Martin F. Nolan, who was concerned that whether December 7, 1941 would "live in infamy" as predicted by President Roosevelt depended on "history":

"One obstacle to history lies in an academic vanguard among the 75 million born between 1945 and 1964. In too many history departments, professors of the baby boomer generation are, as one older historian puts it, 'waiting for veterans to die so revisionism can rule.' "

Revisionist views of history that justify the Japanese bombing of Pearl Harbor, the Bataan death march, and other Japanese atrocities, and condemn the destruction of Hiroshima and Nagasaki, are mischievous and naive.

An article in the *Kansas City Star* by D.M. Giangreco and Kathryn Moore (January 29, 2001) begins:

"The recent completion of the first large-scale production run of Purple Hearts in over half a century has refocused attention on President Harry Truman's decision to drop the atomic bomb on Hiroshima and end World War II.

"Thousands of Purple Hearts — the decoration awarded to U.S. troops wounded in battle — were produced as part of the preparation for an allied invasion of Japan. Heavy casualties were expected.

"Thanks to Truman's decision, the invasion never took place. But the resulting stockpile of Purple Hearts was so large that even today, medals struck in the 1940s are being pinned on the chests of young servicemen and women."

The Bomb was a horrible thing, but so was the great war that it ended.

* * * * *

In Kansas City, Sally Tourtellot was at her desk in the Kansas City Power & Light Company's advertising department when the head of the department stepped out of his office and said:

" 'The war has ended. Leave your work. Go home. Give thanks.' He was crying." *The War Years,* supra.

The advertising staff walked to "the gold dome cathedral" (The Cathedral of the Immaculate Conception) and entered the church with crowds of people coming and going. After prayers of thanks-giving, they walked to 14th and Baltimore where a parade had formed.

"Flags appeared suddenly and some of the people from the hotel bands were marching and playing their instruments. In the hotels along Baltimore people were hanging out of hotel room windows. They were cutting open their feather bed pillows and feathers were floating down like snow."

Later, Sally and her father-in-law went to the Union Station for further celebration:

"High school choirs had gathered in the balconies high up near the ceiling of that grand building. They sang together 'God Bless America,' 'America the Beautiful,' 'The Battle Hymn of the Republic' — and more.

"Everyone was swaying to the music and there wasn't a dry eye in the place." *The War Years*, supra.

In the forgotten CBI Theater, where Tom Thompson still awaited orders returning him to the States, the war's end was greeted with jubilation:

"In the middle of August, we were informed that the Japs had surrendered. The booze flowed everywhere, pilots were firing their Colt 45s into the air, and bedlam continued on into the night." Tom Thompson.

The response by Max Berry at the 117th Station Hospital in the Philippines was more subdued:

"The cease-fire announcement came over the P.A. system in the GI ward where Maj. Bill Dabney and I were making rounds … We quit rounds and joined a sober group of fellow physicians at Headquarters ... I didn't feel jubilant or elated; just sort of numb and God-awful tired." *One Man's WW II*, supra, p. 76.

* * * * *

The Antietem, with Art Doyle's F4U group on board, had just joined the 5th Fleet off Japan when the A-bombs triggered V-J Day. The Antietem was named flagship of the Seventh Fleet — the Asiatic Fleet sometimes known as "MacArthur's Navy" — and hurried to the Yellow Sea to assume command.

CHAPTER EIGHTEEN

Manila

ADMIRAL SPRUANCE and the Fifth Fleet staff prepared to sail for Japan aboard the battleship New Jersey. In the New Jersey's War Log was a one-line entry: "Heard news of the atomic bomb dropped on Hiroshima." Thanks to that bomb, the ship was not leading an invading armada but a victorious occupation force.

The 45,000 ton New Jersey was awesome, a floating, self-propelled fortress populated by 2800 seamen. Her nine 16-inch guns weighed 120 tons each and were capable of lobbing high explosive shells far beyond the horizon. Seven broadsides from the ship's batteries equaled the bomb load of 60 warplanes. Despite her great size, the New Jersey could attain a speed in excess of 33 knots. The New Jersey and her sister ships — the Iowa, the Missouri and the Wisconsin — formed a "fast division" of the world's swiftest battleships. They reigned supreme during the greatest naval war in history but now they were seagoing dinosaurs, doomed by carrier-based air power. (The Iowa-class battleships would all be stricken from the Naval registry later, after fifty years of service.) Flat-tops had come a long way since March 1922 when the rebuilt collier Jupiter became the Navy's first aircraft carrier, hauling aircraft instead of coal. Meanwhile, however, the mighty New Jersey symbolized our victory in the Pacific theater ... an appropriate flagship for the commander of the triumphant Fifth Fleet.

I directed a working party transferring the gear of the staff officers to the battleship. We emptied two B.O.Q.s of their contents, loaded them aboard army trucks, and proceeded to the fleet landing where cargo nets hoisted everything through the air and spewed it out on the New Jersey's fantail. With the aid of a contingent of the ship's stewards' mates and after much sweating and heaving, we finally saw the last of that mountain on the fantail disappear, on its way to living quarters below deck.

* * * * *

The stewards' mates who helped me were the only African-Americans I worked with during all of my Navy days. Admiral Nimitz had not encouraged their assignment to his command because of the "additional problems" of integration, although he favored future elimination of segregation in the service. (*How They Won the War in the Pacific — Nimitz and His Admirals*, page 366, by Edwin P. Hoyt, published by Weybright and Talley, New York).

Captain Redman Callaway's experience was quite different. He developed a camaraderie with most of the black soldiers in his company ..."a certain closeness that comes with shared hardships." And he came to appreciate what his men were able to achieve:

> "My attitudes changed considerably from the stereotyped attitudes I held at the beginning of my command. I saw real accomplishments by these black soldiers, accomplishments made more admirable because they were performed under a constant burden of prejudice."
> *White Captain *** Black Troops*, supra, p.129.

* * * * *

When the long day's work ended, I set out to find my bunkroom. I threaded my way among enlisted men asleep on the teakwood deck, driven from their sleeping compartments by the sultry Guam evening. I walked along narrow passageways, folded in the middle to squeeze through watertight doors, and descended steep, narrow metal ladders. My bunkroom, when I reached it, was hot and crowded, but I located an empty sack and was relieved that somehow a steward's mate had already found his way there with my bags. I stripped down to my skivvies and fell into bed.

* * * * *

The next day I did not watch our departure from Guam's Apra Harbor.

I was busy below deck, preparing for the occupation of Japan. Anticipating victory over Germany as early as 1942, Winston Churchill told the British House of Commons:

"The problems of victory are more agreeable than those of defeat, but they are no less difficult." *A Life in the 20th Century, supra*, page 328.

And aboard the Douglas A. Munro, Communications Officer John Wells pondered an ALNAV message from the Secretary of the Navy, confirming that the war was over but warning that new challenges lay ahead:

"All hands of the United States Navy, Marine Corps and Coast Guard may take satisfaction in the conclusion of the war against Japan and pride in the part played by them in accomplishing that result.

"The demobilization of the armed forces of the United States and the return to conditions of peace will create problems taking patience and control almost as great as the tensions of war. I ask that the discipline which has served so well to bring this democracy through hours of great crisis be maintained to the end that nothing shall mar the record of accomplishments and glory that rightfully belongs to the Navy, the Marine Corps and the Coast Guard." James Forrestal.

The chief of staff for Admiral Spruance, in a pep talk to staff officers, reminded us that our commander had emerged from the Pacific war with a fine reputation, and it was our job to see that this record remained unblemished. The occupation of Japan would be "exacting" but it would also be "a memorable adventure." Motivated, I spent the day helping to organize flag plot.

* * * * *

Our immediate destination was the Philippine Islands, some 1500 miles to the west.

A few days later, at 0600 hours, we entered San Bernardino Strait.

One year before, Japanese warships churned through these waters to attack MacArthur's beachhead on Leyte Gulf, expecting to overwhelm the few guardian American escort carriers and their accompanying destroyers and destroyer escorts. This same strait a few hours later witnessed the disorderly retreat of the Japanese, who had failed to dislodge the American defenders and feared retribution from Admiral Halsey aboard this same New Jersey.

Now the peaceable American Navy hugged the middle of the channel, concerned only with navigational problems.

The water of San Bernardino Strait was a deep blue, with whitecaps cresting the waves. The strait was wide — the island of Samar on the south and the larger Luzon on the north were sometimes nearby, sometimes out of sight. Other points of land rose out of the channel throughout the day. It was a beautiful passage to the city of Manila.

* * * * *

Early the next morning we dropped anchor in historic Manila Bay, one of the finest harbors in the world. In February, American naval units had entered the Bay for the first time since 1942.

The August weather was fickle, with flurries of rain and shafts of sunlight chasing each other over the water. Rain spattered the teakwood deck as our battleship rode like a great, gray ghost in the misty bay. The harbor was obstructed by derelict, strafed and bombed ships resting on the bottom, their superstructures protruding from shallow water … the Hornet's flyers and others took a heavy toll.

Nearby was an Australian cruiser, her three smokestacks amidships rising above a heavily armored hull. A British destroyer flew the familiar Union Jack, her sailors in shorts moving about the deck. Further away, a dilapidated Japanese hospital ship listed to one side, dirty and abandoned. In contrast one of our own hospital ships was anchored close at hand, gleaming white even in the fog.

As I examined Manila's waterfront from shipboard, I made out modern buildings stretching skyward. I was eager to see the beautiful city at close range.

* * * * *

I boarded a boat for the beach. The boat's coxwain expertly held his craft to the side of the ship until his passengers were on the rolling deck, and then set out for a pier near the Manila Hotel.

As we approached the city that I had admired from afar, I discovered that the Philippine capital was devastated. Only Warsaw sustained greater damage, among the martyred cities of the World War II Allies. The pier was a wreck, its roof sagging, its walls half-gone. And those imposing facades along the waterfront hid crumbling, abandoned buildings. The Manila Hotel, where General MacArthur's penthouse was blown up by the Japanese, was now undergoing extensive repair by Army construction crews. Restored rooms were occupied by MacArthur's staff, and sentries denied access to the hotel grounds by all but authorized personnel.

Manila's economy was ravaged by inflation. Japanese occupation currency — pesos and centavos — was now worthless, and U.S. backed Philippine money was in short supply.

Heavy Army vehicles furthered the destruction of streets already in need of major repairs. In contrast were the curious little two-wheeled carts of the Filipinos, pulled by barrel-chested miniature ponies straining at loads many times their weight. Cart drivers harangued servicemen with offers of rides, competing with women on the sidewalks with nothing to offer but themselves.

"Kilroy was here" graffiti boasted that the legendary G.I. of World War II had entered Manila with the initial wave of American forces.

Skinny little girls kept a small ball airborne by kicking it with their ankles. When they saw me watching, they became embarrassed and stopped. However, shyness was a trait foreign to most of Manila's children. They accosted strangers without hesitation, peddled souvenirs aggressively, and bummed handouts from Army messes. In their war-torn city, the assertive child had the best chance of survival.

* * * * *

I visited the Intramurros, the old walled city within Manila, that had endured for nearly four centuries after its construction by Spanish conquistadores … a labyrinth of thick-sided, small-windowed buildings, many of them colleges, churches and missions. Not much remained, for here the Japanese — after blowing up several square miles of the city — had holed up for a last stand two

71

months earlier, and building by building, room by room, were blasted out by the G.I.s.

The Intramurros' 16th century Cathedral of St. Augustine was the oldest church in the Philippines. A survivor of earthquakes and monsoons, the cathedral even now stood sturdily erect amid the ruins. The cathedral bell tower's steps, worn smooth by sextons of centuries past, led to a view of what survived of modern Manila. It would take many years to restore the city to any semblance of her beautiful, pre-war self. Manila and neighboring Corregidor were liberated too late to prevent the death of 100,000 civilians, many of them massacred by Japanese troops who raped, bayoneted, machine-gunned and burned them to death. Like Guam, the Philippines had been joined with the United States in 1898 and, like the Chamorros, the Filipinos had remained loyal to an America half a world away ... and paid dearly.

* * * * *

Grant Hatfield was transferred from Zamboanga to Clark Field outside Manila. While in the city he caught a glimpse of General MacArthur:

"One day I was driving down Rizal Avenue in Manila and saw a big cadillac with five stars on the front and two flags on the bumper. I stopped and, standing on a balcony two stories up, I saw General MacArthur. He was wearing his scrambled egg hat and his sunglasses and was smoking his corn cob pipe with his hands in his hip pockets. What a sight." Grant Hatfield.

Jack O'Hara was also in Manila, assisting in the return of Japanese soldiers to their home islands. From Manila, Jack returned to civilian life; following his Army discharge, he engaged for a time in the advertising business in Kansas City, and then became a highly successful artist in demand for his portraits and landscapes.

CHAPTER NINETEEN

Okinawa and the Kamikazes

ON AUGUST 28, 1945 I boarded the flag ship of Vice Admiral Harry W. Hill's Fifth Amphibious Force ... the massive El Dorado, anchored in Manila Harbor. Admiral Hill had directed amphibious landings on Okinawa from the ship's bridge, and the El Dorado had also served as the command ship for Marine Corps General Holland M. ("Howlin' Mad") Smith during the bloody conquest of Iwo Jima. Perhaps some of my Plattsburg classmates had participated in these assaults from the sea, with nowhere to run or hide if things went wrong.

The El Dorado was equipped with the facilities of a small city, including a printing plant. I was there because of the printing plant ... I carried top secret mine sweeping plans with orders to reproduce their maps of Japanese minefields and return to the New Jersey with 12,000 copies. Marine Staff Sergeant Edwin P. Brodnax accompanied me.

Assaults on shipping had sent most of Japan's navy and merchant marine to the bottom of the sea. Our submarine and carrier attacks had forced the Japanese to route the remainder of their shipping through the Inland Sea and the coastal waters of Japan, where American mines clogged these arteries. An aerial mining campaign by Marianas-based B-29s was particularly destructive; many of the lost Japanese vessels were sunk by American mines in shipping channels and ports. Minefields laid by the Japanese also threatened shipping. Now the Fifth Fleet Mine Force would dispose of these mines, permitting safe passage by occupation forces.

There were all kinds of mines — magnetic, acoustic, pressure. Isolated floating mines menaced shipping lanes around the Pacific and were to be destroyed by gunfire on sight; the minimum safe range was 100 yards.

Magnetic mines were especially troublesome; many were disposed of in "Operation Guinea Pig," allowed to explode against the hulls of ships fitted with sprung decks and manned by volunteer crews. The promise of early discharge from the Navy attracted sailors to this hazardous duty.

* * * * *

During our stay in Manila, the New Jersey moved on to Okinawa. When the minefield charts were ready, we loaded them (a heavy cargo) aboard a PBM Mariner, a Navy flying boat, to fly to Buckner Bay and rejoin the ship. This would be my first time in an airplane, and in six hours we would make the same trip that had taken the New Jersey over two days.

I climbed into the Mariner's gun turret, a glass bubble, and away we went. The loaded plane bumped through the waves, then skimmed along their tops. Soon spray no longer showered the transparent enclosure around my head, and we were airborne.

After we left the island behind, there was nothing to be seen but sky and water; it was a lonely feeling. Okinawa had a land mass of nearly 500 square miles, but in the vast Pacific it seemed a very small needle in a very large haystack. However, the crew were confident of their ability to find the island.

Our arrival at Buckner Bay, Okinawa, recently named for the late General Simon Bolivar Buckner, an Okinawa battle casualty, was sensational. We circled the New Jersey a few times, a signal light blinking identification, and then dropped to the surface of the Bay. The water was rough, and so was the landing … a series of controlled crashes through the waves. By now, several hundred of the New Jersey's crew hung over the ship's rail, consumed by curiosity and expecting a passenger of some note. An ordinary ensign shepherding chart boxes was a disappointment.

The transfer of the cumbersome cargo from plane to small boat to ship in the heavy seas was the only difficult part of the entire operation. But we finally saw the last package aboard and I was home again on the giant battleship.

* * * * *

American forces had landed on Okinawa the Easter Sunday of our "blue network" broadcast. Close to the home island of Kyushu, it was the scene of some of the bloodiest fighting of the Pacific war, the last great battle of World War II. A captured Okinawa would provide a staging base for the invasion of Japan and the island was fanatically defended by the Japanese, over 110,000 of whom died in a futile but devastatingly brutal attempt to forestall invasion. American forces suffered more than 12,000 dead and 36,000 wounded.

During the battle, David Duncan climbed into a plastic-nosed belly tank attached under the wing of a P-38 fighter plane, and photographed the close air support of infantry fighting on the ground.

* * * * *

Off shore, kamikaze pilots pounded our armada of ships. There were over 3000 of these night-and-day suicide attacks — forecasting what to expect from an invasion of the home islands of Japan. The Indianapolis, with Spruance aboard, sustained kamikaze damage; nine of the crew died in the attack.

LST 572 was present during the suicide assaults. It had beached on the island to unload Army engineers and an LCT, and later returned with an Army Signal Service company. The battleship New Mexico was damaged by a kamikaze while close aboard, but LST 572 was not hit. The pilots were after different game.

Clint Kanaga's Elmore was also part of the invasion fleet lying off Okinawa, but was undamaged. The Elmore had carried assault troops for invasions of the Marshall Islands, Guam, Pelilieu, the Philippines, and other Pacific hot spots — twenty-four islands in all. Clint went ashore on most of the landings. Now, after discharging troops at Okinawa and observing kamikaze assaults for three days, the unscathed Elmore withdrew … its mission accomplished.

Neil Lombardi's St. Louis was part of the Okinawa fleet:

"There were lots of kamikazes while we were at Okinawa, but they expended most of their force against the outlying groups of destroyers, the 'picket ships,' and those that struggled through were fairly easy targets." *Some Reminiscences of World War Two*, supra, p.23.

To counter the deadly kamikazes, the picket ships were set up around the island. When bogies (enemy aircraft) appeared on a picket's radar screen, the destroyer summoned American flyers to intercept. A high percentage of the enemy were shot down before reaching the island.

Not all of the suicide planes failed in their mission, however. Bob Hanger witnessed a successful kamikaze attack:

"April 1, 1945. Several of us were hanging on the rail of our troop transport watching the amphibious landing at Okinawa, just 350 miles from Japan. Suddenly, a lone Japanese aircraft sails over us not much more than mast high and so quiet it appeared to be gliding. There's no shooting from the airplane or the ships; the plane seems to hang suspended for a few seconds, then disappears.

"Before we can even begin to wonder what's going on, there's a tremendous explosion as the suicide airplane hits the troop transport Hinsdale squarely amidships. We learn later that the ship didn't sink, but the 3rd battalion Second Marines lost eight dead and 37 wounded. Ironically, these were the first casualties of the campaign, inflicted on troops which did not participate in the landing. This was our first experience with Kamikaze, the Heavenly Wind, but not our last." *Who's Gonna Live?*, supra, p. 45.

* * * * *

The cruiser Birmingham, with Wally Burger on board, was part of the Okinawa armada. It had departed the mainland in early February and arrived at Okinawa in late March after participating in the Iwo Jima battle and a stop at the giant fleet anchorage at Ulithli.

On May 4, still off Okinawa, Wally left his bunkroom for a cup of coffee just as his roommate entered. The Birmingham ship's history describes what happened next:

"Aboard the Birmingham everything seemed rather peaceful. It was a beautiful, cloudless day, and we weren't firing at the moment. Then, at 0840, a plane was splashed by the St.Louis only 4000 yards away. The very next thing that most of us recall was the rattling sound of 20 m.m. fire coming from our own ship, and to men who had fought and lived through almost constant air attacks for forty consecutive days and nights, 20 m.m. fire was the most frightening God-awful sound imaginable. The next few seconds seemed like an eternity, and then it happened." *CL 62: The Saga of the USS Birmingham.*

A kamikaze plane struck the Birmingham, missing the bridge but demolishing the bunkrooms and sick bay. It killed Wally's roommate as well as one hundred more of the ship's crew including the Birmingham's two doctors. Wally Burger was unharmed.

* * * * *

The crew of the Lucky Luce, one of the picket ships, hoped that their good fortune would continue, but on May 4 their luck ran out. When a kamikaze scored a near miss, the resulting explosion knocked out the destroyer's electrical system. The Luce's guns were affected, and additional kamikazes got through to sink the ship. She went to the bottom in three minutes, losing forty percent of her crew.

The Luce, after a brief twenty-three months' service, would fight no more.

Cliff Jones survived the sinking:

"The water came up and just floated me off. I started swimming the breast stroke." Cliff Jones.

LCMs, dubbed "pallbearers" by destroyer sailors, routinely tracked the picket ships to pick up survivors of sinkings, and one of these fished Cliff out of the sea.

Cliff Jones returned to Kansas City for thirty days' survivor's leave and a new assignment. After the war, Cliff became chairman and president of R.B. Jones, the seventh largest insurance broker in the United States, and later founded the mutual funds management company of Jones & Babson in partnership with former Navy flyer Alfred J. Hoffman.

Rejection of my earlier requests for destroyer duty was fortuitous. The toll of kamikaze attacks in the Pacific war: 157 destroyers, 4907 dead sailors, and 4832 wounded sailors. Page 3. *The Sacrificial Lambs*, William Sholin, 1989, Mountain View Books, Bonney Lake, Wash.

* * * * *

One day in early September, I visited this island for which Americans and Japanese alike had paid so dearly. I was accompanied by Navy Lieutenants Don Chaney of Fairport Harbor, Ohio, and Robert K. Hage of New York City.

Naha, the capital city of Okinawa, was a rubbish heap, smelling like a dynamited stone quarry. The river outside the city was choked and stinking. But the hills overlooking Naha, once battlefields where the Japanese commander had made his stand, were now quiet, green and deceptively alluring.

We climbed a slope behind the ruined city. Despite the terraced terrain, the ascent was difficult. Rank grass concealed numerous holes, and occasional mushy marshland. Dwarf pines with sharp needles grew close together like hedgerows to form impenetrable thickets, forcing us to find our way around them. It was a battleground that had favored the defenders. And the victory was costly:

"The battle for Okinawa had ended in another overwhelming American victory. An entire Japanese army had been destroyed, together with hundreds of planes and the greatest battleship of the Imperial Navy. Yet few Americans who took part in the campaign felt any sense of exultation when it was over. The general feeling was one of anxiety and dread before the tasks that lay ahead. If the capture of a base in the Ryukus had been this bad, what would the assault on Japan itself be like?" *Eagle Against the Sun*, supra, page 540.

Tombs and burial vaults burrowed into hillsides. They contained shrines of glazed pottery, and urns holding the ashes of the dead. The tombs had been used by the enemy as pillboxes, and when I stopped beside one of them I looked down at my feet to discover the remains of a Japanese soldier who had holed up there. And there he died, in a small black opening in the ground.

We returned to the harbor and re-entered a familiar world of noise and dust generated by industrious Americans.

Grant Hatfield ended his Army career on Okinawa, his dental office in the back of a truck. Grant returned to Kansas City and a civilian dentistry practice in more orthodox surroundings.

* * * * *

While we were anchored in Buckner Bay, the formal surrender of Japan occurred aboard the New Jersey's sister ship, the Missouri. The New Jersey, Admiral Spruance's flagship, was a more appropriate surrender site, but the President of the United States was from Missouri and the ceremony was held aboard the battleship named for his native state. Admiral Spruance remained on the New Jersey instead of proceeding to Tokyo Bay to witness the momentous event. We wondered why.

The Seventh Fleet's Task Force 72 was off the China coast when the surrender occurred. It included the flagship USS Antietem, two other carriers, and six destroyers. At first, surly Japanese declared that the Emperor's surrender did not apply to Shanghai, but their prisoners were soon released. It was a memorable day for Art Doyle:

"On September 2, 1945, we flew a rooftop 'show of strength' at first light over Shanghai and continued with five more during the day — causing the Japs to lay down their guns, open prison gates and release POWs, one of whom, a radioman, was able to get on our frequency shortly after noon and broadcast to us a dramatic hour long account of the day's happenings on the ground. We had a good day, but MacArthur had a better one aboard the USS Missouri in Tokyo Bay, Japan." Arthur Doyle.

CHAPTER TWENTY

Wakanoura and the POWs

A FEW DAYS LATER, the New Jersey left Okinawa for Japan. All was serene as our bow sheared the waves like a broadsword. The sea tumbled alongside, slid past the steel flanks of the ship, and closed in our wake. We were accompanied by plenty of sunshine and salt spray, and a few flying fish.

The occupation of Japan was just beginning. How hostile were the defeated Japanese? The Fifth Fleet preparations on Guam had been dual in nature, for invasion as well as for occupation. This voyage would have been much different had the New Jersey been the flagship of an assault force, sailing against an entire population ready to die for their emperor in a final, suicidal fight.

During the voyage a seaplane was launched by catapult — an OS2U Kingfisher. William H. Dunn Sr., a Kansas Citian who would later head one of the nation's largest construction enterprises, was a Kingfisher pilot during the war:

"The Kingfisher was a single-engine seaplane used for scout observation, as well as directing ship-to-shore gunfire, and it was also used to tow a sleeve for gunnery practice. There was nothing glamorous about this airplane with its cruising speed of only 130 knots, and most of its scouting flights at an altitude of 500 feet. The plane was attached to cruisers and battleships, and launched from a powder-activated catapult ... usually the most thrilling part of flying the Kingfisher, since the plane accelerated to 100 miles per hour in 90 feet. It landed in the water after the cruiser or battleship made a quick 90-degree turn, creating a slick area for landing that lasted for about 30-seconds. The slick was needed, since the waves many times were eight to ten feet in height. A hook dropped from the deck of the ship then lifted the plane back on deck." William H. Dunn.

I watched the reclamation of the Kingfisher from the sea. The plane was a sitting duck for enemy fighters. Bill Dunn was told by a Pensacola flight instructor that if he ever saw a Japanese Zero he should fly about five feet above the water in the hope of escaping detection. "Otherwise, it would be the end of the road for a pilot flying a Kingfisher."

After an extensive training period, Dunn received orders to report to the battleship Wisconsin just as the war ended.

* * * * *

Meanwhile, flying off the Antietem, Bostonian Art Doyle had another memorable day:

"On September 9, 1945, the Japs surrendered their occupation of Korea. I led a four plane formation of F4Us at low level over a mass of humanity that surrounded the Capitol Building in Seoul. We swept in from the South, identified the Capitol (looked like the Boston

State House, per Naval Intelligence), went into close echelon formation and flew a tight circle around the dome. While we circled, the Jap flag over the Capitol was lowered and the American flag was raised! It was a thrill and a half to witness. " Arthur Doyle.

* * * * *

Instead of proceeding straight to Tokyo Bay we made first for Kii Suido, a channel between the islands of Shikoku and Honshu leading to the Inland Sea of Japan. The sweep areas mapped by my mine charts included this channel, heavily guarded during the war, and we sailed through a passage only recently cleared by minesweepers.

The New Jersey dropped anchor in Wakanoura Wan, a bay bordering the small resort community of Wakanoura, on Honshu. Wakanoura boasted some of the most beautiful coastal scenery in Japan.

* * * * *

We were there because the nearby port city of Wakayama was a major embarkation point for newly liberated prisoners of war, who were in bad shape. The bushido contempt for surrender, exhibited by the Japanese soldiers on Manus and Guam, dictated inhumane treatment for POWs in the Pacific — in the eyes of Japanese captors, their disgraced prisoners deserved to die:

"The Japanese were not directly genocidal in their POW camps. They did not herd their white prisoners into gas chambers and burn their corpses in ovens. But they drove them toward mass death just the same. They beat them until they fell, then beat them for falling, beat them until they bled, then beat them for bleeding. They denied them medical treatment. They starved them. When the International Red Cross sent food and medicine, the Japanese looted the shipments. They sacrificed prisoners in medical experiments. They watched them die by tens of thousands from diseases of malnutrition like beriberi, pellagra, and scurvy, and from epidemic tropical diseases: malaria, dysentery, tropical ulcers, cholera. Those who survived could only look ahead to being worked to death. If the war had lasted another year, there would not have been a POW left alive. *Prisoners of the Japanese — POWs of World War II in the Pacific*, by Gavan Daws, William Morrow and Company, Inc., New York, N.Y., 1994.

The Instrument of Surrender signed a few days before our arrival commanded the Imperial Government and the Imperial General Headquarters to liberate all prisoners of war and "provide for their protection, care, maintenance and immediate transportation to places as directed." The Japanese were cooperative in the evacuation, atoning somewhat for the misery inflicted upon their captives.

We encountered no problems in the Wakayama area, where thousands of freed prisoners were welcomed by sympathetic compatriots:

"Brass bands. Speeches from generals. Coffee and doughnuts and ice cream and Coke from Red Cross girls. White hospital ships, shining bright, with wonderful names, Samaritan, Hope, Rescue, Relief ..." *Prisoners of the Japanese*, supra, p.343.

Just as we arrived, one of those hospital ships departed. Admiral Spruance asked the New Jersey's band to play as the big white vessel passed us, and everyone cheered during the few moments when the ships were side by side. These were moments of pride on the part of all of us ... pride in the mighty battleship, symbol of our naval power, and pride in the Americans who could still muster a cheer after surviving the prison camps.

* * * * *

I accompanied an inspection team of three senior staff officers ashore at Wakanoura.

Once our small boat docked, we climbed onto a long, concrete pier. Blue-uniformed policemen gravely saluted us. Civilians, including children, stopped and bowed solemnly as we passed them. Uncertain of the proper protocol, we acknowledged them with casual nods. The first Allied forces had landed here only three days before, and we were an unaccustomed sight.

We passed expressionless Japanese soldiers and sailors. The Instrument of Surrender had commanded military and naval personnel to remain at their posts and to continue to perform non-combatant duties. A short month ago we had been at war with these people. I wondered how they felt about us. Did they fear us? Should we fear them?

Life, and death, went on in the village. Rattling, pre-war Fords served as taxis, and an old streetcar clanged along the main thoroughfare. But the principal mode of transportation was the bicycle, and sedate, dignified men pumped along on them, their wives riding sidesaddle on the rear fender.

A funeral procession trudged past us, headed by three civilians walking abreast. The man in the center bore the boxed ashes of the deceased, while his flankers carried small saplings. Behind followed other mourners, their demeanor placid, stoic … I tried in vain to identify any bereaved kin. It was common for demobilized soldiers to return with the ashes of deceased comrades, and perhaps these were such remains.

The houses and shops of Wakanoura were insubstantial, made of wood and paper, with open balconies and thin walls. All were perched on hillsides, as were the cemeteries ("They must bury their dead standing up" commented one of my companions). The buildings had been spared the harsher consequences of war, but the pretty little village had given up sons to die in jungles and bleak island caves.

The Japanese fastidiously removed their shoes outside a hotel entrance and added them to a row of unattended footwear lining the walk. A curiosity then, this became a familiar sight. The hotel was the site for processing liberated prisoners of war before they boarded hospital ships.

A businesslike detachment of Canadian troops was just pulling out as we passed. Now the town would belong to the Marines, and I watched curious children crowding around a Marine sentry — staring at his bayonet, his carbine, his knife. The weapons of American fighting men were no threat to them. The Marines would also soon withdraw, leaving Wakanoura once more in the possession of its Japanese inhabitants.

We climbed to the top of a neighboring hill and looked down on a small fishing village in the next valley. Its fragile houses were huddled close together, with barely enough room for a footpath between them. But we also saw rifle pits, barbed wire, and dugouts, all commanding the beach. Invasion, even in this isolated area, would have been a bloody business.

Wakayama lay only a few miles to the north, but we had no time to visit it. A B-29 raid had destroyed much of that city. Having viewed the flimsy buildings of Wakanoura, I could imagine the loss of life from that attack.

We returned to the pier and reboarded the New Jersey.

* * * * *

Later, on September 25, the Elmore brought occupation troops to Wakayama, but Clint Kanaga was no longer aboard:

"We came home to Seattle after Okinawa and I called Colonel Roberts at Lejeune to see if he could get me off the ship — twenty-one months was enough. He told me that they (the whole Marine Corps six divisions) were going to Japan. I said 'Fine — I've had it easy so please get me with you.' He said 'OK.'

However, Clint never got to Japan:

"On my way home before going to Lejeune, Truman dropped the two bombs and the war was over." Clint Kanaga.

* * * * *

When the war ended, Bob Hanger's Marine outfit was dispatched to the Nagasaki area, to survey the manufacturing capability of the little town of Isahaya. The Marines established their camp about ten miles out of town and then set out for Isahaya. Like our inspection team at Wakayama, they weren't sure just what to expect:

"On the first trip, our party consisted of me, my executive officer, First Sergeant, Gunnery Sergeant, and a dozen marines, all of us armed to the teeth. We had fought these people so long and so bitterly that it was difficult to imagine traveling ten miles without a conflict. When our convoy (one jeep, one 6 X 6 truck) took off, the event had the overtones of a suicide mission.

"The Japanese were more nervous than we were, and with good reason since we were the conquerors. We went through a couple of villages on the way to our destination, both with narrow streets and overhanging buildings, both with women and children scrambling for cover and men (many of them still in uniform) who simply turned their backs. Tense." *Who's gonna live?* supra, page 51.

The people of Isahaya, when the expedition reached it, were equally apprehensive. But there were no problems.

CHAPTER TWENTY-ONE

The Occupation of Japan Begins

FROM WAKANOURA WAN, the New Jersey proceeded to Tokyo Bay, arriving September 18, 1945. The 4th Marine Division had landed 9000 Marines here nineteen days earlier to begin the Allied occupation of Japan.

Admiral Halsey, Third Fleet commander, awaited us aboard the battleship Missouri. Halsey once promised to ride the Japanese emperor's white horse through the streets of Tokyo, and the Navy's code name for Halsey's Tokyo Bay entry was "White Horse." The Missouri, stage for the September 2 surrender ceremony, flew a much-traveled American flag that had witnessed the surrender proceedings — the same flag had flown above the American Capitol on December 7, 1941 and more recently was raised over Berlin during Truman's Pottsdam visit in July.

Admiral Nimitz participated in the surrender formalities, conducted by General Douglas MacArthur. Nimitz was initially irritated by President Truman's choice of MacArthur for this role, feeling that the Navy had been slighted, but he was mollified by the selection of a Navy ship as the site of the ceremony.

The proceedings were photographed by David Douglas Duncan, a prized opportunity. Duncan was aboard because the officer in charge of press arrangements chanced to be an old comrade-in-arms:

"Commodore Fitzhugh Lee received me almost immediately, although for sure he did not place my name until we were again face to face ...

"How could anybody have my luck!

"He explained graciously and carefully that he was being besieged by the biggest guns from Washington to London to Paris and even Moscow, to get their representatives aboard. That was at the government level. At the press level he was being depth-charged around the clock. While telling me this he kept right on working at his desk, writing. Then he stood up again and handed me a card with a lean smile. 'Don't worry! You're aboard. Surely no man here deserves it more than a United States Marine.' " *Yankee Nomad,* supra, pp.194-5.

David Duncan's vantage point for a priceless photograph of the surrender ceremony was the best:

"I was upon a five-inch gun turret, back slightly from the deck ... just below me a catwalk connected the captain's quarters with the lower deck, where the surrender documents waited ... A moment later, to my astonishment, General MacArthur and Admiral Halsey walked out on the catwalk right beneath me. Commodore Fitzhugh Lee really fixed me up royally. I certainly wasn't the person closest to the surrender signing table. But I did have one of the greatest overall views of the momentous pageant taking place aboard that battleship." *Yankee Nomad,* supra, page 195.

After the war, David Douglas Duncan became a free-lance journalist who roamed the world. He covered the war in Korea, was photo-correspondent for *LIFE Magazine* and ABC-TV during the Vietnam War, and was given the Robert Capa Award for valor as a photo-journalist. He was twice named Photographer of the Year by the American Society of Magazine Photographers, photographed Presidential Conventions for NBC-TV, exhibited his work in art museums, and has written several books. An archive of his work has been established at the Harry Ransom Humanities Research Center, The University of Texas at Austin.

* * * * *

Halsey and his ships were relieved by our Fifth Fleet. During the two-day interval between our arrival and Halsey's departure, there was amassed in the harbor off the city of Yokosuka much of the naval might of the Pacific Fleet. It was a show of force, accompanied by daily air reconnaissance flights, to insure the release of prisoners of war and to confirm the continued disarming of Japan.

In the quickly organized officers' club at the Yokosuka naval base, the members of the Bull's flotilla celebrated their impending voyage home. Among the celebrants was Navy Lieutenant Robert McCarty of Kansas City, whose battleship the USS Pennsylvania was involved in many Pacific island campaigns. Then, on September 20, the ships of the Third Fleet weighed anchor and steamed out of the harbor. Pennants fluttered from mastheads, and stars and yards of ribbon trailed out behind fantails. Bands blared from the departing ships' decks as they slid past the silent New Jersey, where we enviously watched and told ourselves that one day we too would be going home.

* * * * *

It was already tourist season in Yokosuka. The merchants of the town, encouraged by the arrival of American seamen and Yankee dollars, shrugged off their defeat and prepared to profit from post-war occupation. Shore patrolmen insured law and order while sailors from the ships in the harbor searched the streets for souvenirs and entertainment. Beer, not allowed aboard ship, was available in a GI beer garden for all enlisted personnel, in downtown Yokosuka — three cans of beer for ten yen. Rickshaw rides were a popular pastime, as blue jackets on liberty were drawn through the streets by Japanese half their size.

Inflation plagued post-war Japan. The official rate of exchange —yen for U.S. dollars — bore little relation to black market (yama-ichi) reality. Many Japanese merchants would not deal in yen at all, insisting upon bartering. A carton of American cigarettes was a cheap price to pay for a silk kimono, and servicemen took their chances with the illegal swaps. There was added appeal in owning something acquired on the black market ... the forbidden traffic had entertainment value.

The New Jersey's paymaster redeemed yen aboard ship at the official rate of exchange, an unrealistic fifteen to the dollar. Around the corner from the paymaster's office, a sailor discreetly offered thirty yen for a dollar. Enterprising seamen made a nice profit by moving between the two, doubling their money.

Ashore, pearls were popular. Sources ranged from the army PX to black market operatives. There were bargains on the black market for those who were able to judge quality, and minor disasters awaiting those who were not. Good buys in clothing were available to servicemen in the PX, where T shirts were 35 cents each, and dress shoes, rationed in the States, $5.50 a pair.

* * * * *

Almost a century earlier Commodore Matthew Perry had negotiated the Treaty of Kanagawa, prying open an isolated empire to Western trade. Western technology followed, and within fifty years Japan was a world power. In his scholarly portrayal of post-surrender Japan (*Embracing Defeat*, 1999,

W.W. Norton & Company, Inc., NY, NY), John W. Dower wrote:

> "In 1853, a modest fleet of four vessels, two of them coal-burning 'black ships,' had arrived to force the country open. In 1945, a huge, glistening armada came back to close it." (page 19)

Militarism had remained a part of Japanese culture, with the samurai warrior held in high esteem. And although there was a veneer of democracy, Emperor Hirohito was the revered head of a feudal Japan.

Hirohito, a small, myopic man with a wispy mustache, appeared anything but menacing even when mounted on his large, white charger. Nevertheless, Japanese fighting men cheering their man-god were a frequent spectacle in wartime newsreel films.

After almost four years of warfare, the average American knew the Japanese only as enemies with an alien culture. Language is the heart of culture, but for me the Japanese language was indecipherable and unpronounceable; I despaired of progressing beyond "sayonara" (good-bye) and "arigato" (thank you). And Japanese writing, with its thousands of strange characters, was hopeless.

Only a few thousand Allied troops occupied Japan, a nation of eighty million people. American occupation policy relied upon the civil behavior of the conquered Japanese. That assessment of the Japanese character proved to be accurate, for in response to American authority they were docile. Nowhere to be seen were the bloodthirsty "Japs" caricatured in American wartime cartoons. The monsters who terrorized the Pacific vanished. Although Hirohito's command to surrender provoked a brief insurrection by a few military extremists, virtually all of Japan capitulated without protest. The Japanese military were disarmed and discharged by the occupation forces. There was no guerrilla activity. We were safe in a tranquil country ... "The moment the war ended the Japanese changed, like traffic lights turning from red to green." *Prisoners of the Japanese*, supra, p. 347.

On the day of the surrender ceremony, a St.Louis newspaper corespondent in Tokyo wrote:

> "Tokyo was quiet and undemonstrative today as Japanese civilians gradually adjusted themselves to the fact that they had lost the war." *St.Louis Daily News*, September 2, 1945.

The writer described Japanese soldiers staring impassively as American soldiers and vehicles passed. A surrender that came as a complete shock was nevertheless accepted calmly: "The most amazing thing is the lack of concern, even lack of curiosity, displayed by many of the Japanese ..."

* * * * *

Railways still operated throughout the country, and I made my first trip outside Yokosuka aboard a Japanese electric train, to the small community of Kita Kamakura, just one train station stop north of the larger, feudal Kamakura.

Here, as in Wakanoura, Americans were a novelty and I was treated with formal courtesy. I bought a few inexpensive souvenirs and wandered through narrow streets. I also examined religious structures — temples, shrines, and Buddhas of various sizes and descriptions — being careful to avoid any sign of disrespect. The inhabitants stared, but with curiosity, not hostility. The children hid themselves from the large, round-eyed stranger.

CHAPTER TWENTY-TWO

The Fujiya and Tokyo

AFTER TWO WEEKS at anchor in Tokyo Bay, I accompanied two other staff officers on an inspection trip to the isolated mountain country southwest of Tokyo. Our destination was a resort hotel, the Fujiya. We were joined in our station wagon by an interpreter and an armed Marine driver ... we would be the first occupation force to visit this remote area.

* * * * *

Among the Marines in distant Isahaya, caution remained the watchword:

"It soon became evident that a show of force was no longer necessary, if, indeed, it ever had been, but the official position was still the same: no mingling with the Japanese and continue to travel armed and ready to fight. We complied by staying away from towns except in the line of duty, and by traveling in enough force to discourage opposition.

"This meant, among other things, that our visits to Isahaya always included at least a truckload and a jeep load of marines, never less than twenty, armed and helmeted. Arms and helmets were not much in evidence, however, and the trips were looked upon, by our men, as very good duty. Consequently, the order to travel in strength actually served to hasten fraternization." *Who's gonna live?* supra, page 52-53.

That autumn, Bob Hanger accumulated enough discharge points to ship home. He returned to Kansas City and a successful advertising career.

* * * * *

Our little expedition went first to Yokohama to pick up a military pass.

Japanese highway traffic followed the left-hand side of the road. American troops stepped aside at the toot of our horn, but Japanese cyclists and pedestrians were oblivious to our approach. Accidents were averted by the narrowest of margins along the crowded route.

In Yokohama we saw the devastating effect of B-29 bombs. Crowded and built with highly inflammable wood and paper, the city had been exceptionally vulnerable to incendiary attack; vast numbers of civilians died in fire storms. Eighty percent of Yokohama was destroyed in a single raid. Some buildings remained standing, but their fallen, dismembered neighbors lay about them. From a desert of broken masonry and charred wood was rising a shantytown of corrugated iron shacks.

Why all the uproar over the atom bomb? How could the "nuked" Hiroshima and Nagasaki have been more ravaged than this? As Andy Rooney wrote:

"In the fury over the atomic bombs we dropped on Hiroshima and Nagasaki in August, historians have tended to minimize the force with which we were already hitting Tokyo and other places in Japan. In May and June alone in 1945, bombers based on Pacific islands and fighter planes from aircraft carriers were dropping huge bomb tonnages on Japan. If anyone thinks Nagasaki and Hiroshima were our only targets, they should be reminded that our B-29s bombed thirty-nine Japanese cities in the spring of 1945. *My War*, supra, pp 298-9.

American strategists in World War II believed that moderation in war was a betrayal of those asked to fight it. America backed its fighting men with all of the resources and weapons at its disposal … prepared to bomb the Japanese "back to the stone age." *Over Here*, supra. The cessation of hostilities did not leave combatants wondering why they had risked their lives in an ambivalent conflict ... their country clearly wanted to win this one, and war ended in total victory.

We viewed the ruins at Yokohama with considerable awe but little sympathy. In a letter home, I later wrote that "After Manila, this scene of devastation roused no gentle emotion." B-san (Mr. B), as the Japanese respectfully called the lethal B-29s, had done a thorough job.

* * * * *

At the Shore Patrol office, a lieutenant commander issued our pass and we departed.

We traveled more crowded highways, flanked by more bomb damage. Ruins were commonplace.

At last we began to pass through open country, and the desolation was behind us.

We were often in sight of the seashore, and fishing boats. In coastal indentations, rude fences made of stakes formed oyster beds and from this homely source came pearls! Inland, men in loin cloths, with nets and seines, waded the rivers.

The road gradually gained altitude, and tea plantations appeared on terraced hillsides. Soon the source of Japan's silk industry could be seen on the mountain slopes — mulberry trees in neat rows.

Below us in the valleys were streams, rushing over rocks and under bridges to the sea. Spinning in the grip of these foaming cascades were wooden water wheels. Some of Japan's utilities still functioned, and the water was harnessed to generate hydroelectric power.

The higher we climbed, the more rugged and beautiful the scenery.

When we arrived at Miyanoshita, an old-fashioned spa town and the site of the sprawling Fujiya, a polite hotelier wasn't sure what to expect. His hotel, once frequented by wealthy tourists from Europe and America, more recently had been the refuge of unemployed Axis diplomats and displaced aristocrats, but if any guests remained they were invisible. In the hotel register were the names of visitors from Germany and Italy, as well as Sweden — exiles living comfortably in a Western-style hotel built in 1878 whose ground floor included three steam baths, a white-tiled swimming pool, a Western-style bar, a library with stacks of old books, and a beautiful dining room.

We photographed two smiling, kimono-clad hotel employees, rewarding them with occupation currency … a pack of American cigarettes worth thirty yen (about $2.00) on the Yokosuka black market.

As we stood beside the dusty station wagon lunching on dry rations, the hotel manager appeared with cups of tea. This gesture was unexpected; our picnic on his doorstep was an intrusion.

Following lunch, we visited nearby Lake Hakone, a gemlike body of water ringed by stately old fir trees. On a clear day Mount Fujiyama was visible across the lake, but clouds now veiled Japan's most famous landmark.

A village hugged the north end of the lake. We passed a frowning Caucasian in a white shirt and navy blue trousers, and several blonde hikers traveled the village road … perhaps they were fugitives from the Fujiya. Their presence in this mountain fastness was puzzling but hardly threatening.

86

A famous old Shinto shrine lay on the lakeshore just beyond the village. Its approach was lined by giant fir trees planted centuries before ... many generations of Japanese had worshipped in this place. On a box-like altar inside the door worshippers offered oblations. Despite Japan's acute paper shortage, I was able to find a post card that depicted the scene. Although most Japanese were Buddhists, the government-sponsored cult of state Shintoism was a powerful force in Japan. More shamanism than religion, it fostered the concepts of Japanese racial superiority and the sanctity of the Emperor. The creed had reinforced the Japanese war effort and would soon be abolished.

Our return trip led through the shrine city of Hase, near Kamakura, with its great bronze Buddha (Daibutsu) dating back to the 13th century. The brooding figure towered almost forty feet above us, the largest Buddha in all of Japan.

* * * * *

The following week — as tourists, not conquerors — we rode an express train to Tokyo. It was dilapidated, but swift. The few seats were at a premium.

The Japanese pushed and wriggled their way aboard, their elbows at the ready, and then bore the cramped discomfort of the ride with the stoicism of people who expected no better.

The passengers' clothing was shabby. Many of the women were dressed in "mompei," working trousers, and others wore kimonos. The Japanese military turned over uniforms (heitai fuku), as well as supplies, to the civilian population soon after the cessation of hostilities; discarded uniforms, renamed "haisen fuku" (defeat suits), would be the warmest clothing available to the Japanese when winter arrived.

After two hours, our train arrived at the Tokyo railroad station, an old red brick building that had lost its top story in an air raid earlier in the year. Passengers pushed and shoved to escape the confines of the cars, and we were swept into the October sunlight of the railway platform.

* * * * *

From the station, we walked to the Ginza, a modern thoroughfare disfigured by bomb-damage. Japanese vendors conducted business out of suitcases and carts. Whenever we stopped to examine their merchandise, a crowd of the curious collected instantly, standing on tiptoe, craning their necks to watch the transaction with the Americans.

On one corner, a ragged fellow sat cross-legged on the sidewalk, cobbling together boots from canvas leggings and composition soles.

Despite occasional G.I. adventures, the black market was primarily for the Japanese. In Tokyo, territory was allocated among gangs and one group controlled the Ginza area. Sometimes people would disperse at our approach, leaving black market operatives hastily stuffing merchandise into bags. As soon as we passed by, they returned to business — clearly we were no threat, despite the uniforms.

The Tokyo Chamber of Commerce sponsored a bazaar in a large department store, catering to the occupation forces. The shop had little to offer ... straw hats, cosmetics, and cheap pictures. Starving, threadbare Japan contrasted greatly with the abundance of America, a cornucopia despite the years of total war effort.

The medieval palace grounds of the Emperor lay in a park, protected by a wide moat containing fat carp and a high stone wall several centuries old. The ancient stone work was imposing — great slabs, somehow hauled to the site and then shaped and fitted together with painstaking precision.

Beyond the wall the emperor's unimpressive residence was largely intact. In March, 1945, Tokyo was decimated by the most destructive bombing raid in history — a firestorm fanned by high winds consumed much of the city — and by June magnesium cluster bombs and napalm had wiped out 56.3 square miles of the Japanese capital. Inside the imperial palace grounds some buildings were set on fire, but our bombers avoided destroying Hirohito's palace. Now a cooperative emperor facilitated peaceful occupation of the country.

MacArthur's headquarters occupied the nearby six-story Dai Ichi building, one of the few structures still intact. From this fortress-like building, the Supreme Commander Allied Powers (SCAP) was managing the affairs of Japan.

We walked past movie theatres where long queues of people patiently waited to enter. The Japanese too found temporary escape in celluloid romances. But the oriental matinee idols pictured on the theatre walls were strangers and the Japanese characters on the marquees meant nothing to us.

* * * * *

Close by the palace was the Diet building, home of the Japanese bicameral legislature and Japan's most visible concession to democratic government. Completed just nine years earlier, it too had been spared by B-san. We were greeted politely at the entrance by a well-dressed Japanese gentleman who spoke fluent English and offered to serve as our guide.

We were escorted to the chamber where the House of Peers met three months out of every year. A special dais in the front of the room, rising high above the floor, supported a golden throne where Hirohito sat on those occasions when he was to address the Peers.

Our guide compared the Diet to the United States Congress. There had been an elected parliament throughout the war years, but Japan's rulers had only paid lip-service to their legislative body.

We had lunch in Tokyo's Imperial Hotel, designed by Frank Lloyd Wright in the 1920s. One wing had been demolished by a bomb. Service by a well-trained staff was excellent. The bill of fare was uninspired but the price was right, a scant ten yen (sixty-seven cents).

We returned to the railway station. Promptly at the appointed time the car doors slammed shut and it was standing room only, all the way back to Yokosuka.

* * * * *

In October, 1945, Gordon Robertson returned to the continental United States to marry Frances Hodges of Olathe, Kansas, a winsome young lady he met at a church dance while an aviation cadet. He remained in the Navy as a career officer. In February, 1967, after a variety of assignments with ever-increasing responsibilities, he became commanding officer of his old ship, the USS Hornet. In June of that year, he made the 100,000th landing on the carrier's flight deck. In 1969, Gordon retired to Kansas City with the rank of captain, ending twenty-seven years of eventful, distinguished Navy service.

Maxwell Berry, now a lieutenant colonel with a bronze star medal for meritorious achievement in connection with military operations against the enemy as well as a highly regarded tropical medicine consultant, also left for home. "Finally, in late October, 1945, two thousand of us boarded the most beautiful ship in the world: the one which carried us home." *One Man's WW II,* supra, p.77. Once back in Kansas City, Dr. Berry resumed his medical practice. He also served as a clinical professor of medicine at both the University of Kansas School of Medicine and the University of Missouri-Kansas City medical school and was honored by his peers as a Master of the American College of Physicians.

The final months of 1945, Task Force 72 patrolled the Yellow Sea area. Wartime alliances with the Chinese and the Russians were crumbling, and another Communist country, North Korea, in five years would launch a new conflict by invading its neighbor to the south. All of these powers converged where the Task Force was stationed, and its presence in that corner of the world was significant. Surveillance flights by Art Doyle and the other carrier pilots were an important part of that presence.

Officers of Bombing Squadron Two, a much-decorated group. Gordon Robertson, far right, second row.
Photo courtesy of Gordon H. Robertson

Gordon Robertson brings his Helldiver home after New Guinea bombing mission.
April 22, 1944
Photo courtesy of Gordon H. Robertson

USS Hornet (CV-12) — it replaced General Jimmy Doolittle's "Shangri La" (CV-8)
Photo courtesy of Gordon H. Robertson

Hornet scoreboard and Squadron Commanding Officers
with Hornet's Captain (third from left) — October 1944
Photo courtesy of Gordon H. Robertson

Bill Deramus was Trainmaster of India's Bengal and Assam Railway, working under rough conditions and doing a transportation job "unequalled in history."

The Railway brought supplies for China, flown over the "Hump" by F.L. (Tom) Thompson in his "Dumbo," below.

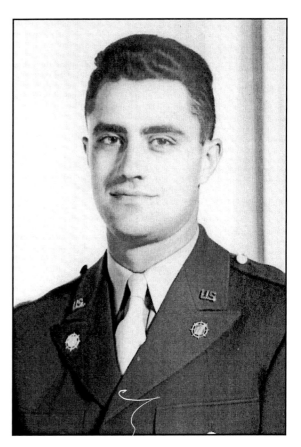

Major William Deramus
Photo courtesy of Jean Deramus

"Dumbo"
The Curtiss-Wright C-46 Commando was the largest twin reciprocating engine transport ever built.
Photo courtesy of F.L. Thompson

Beer Bust, Saipan, December 1944 — Robert C. Hanger, standing third from left.
A highly successful effort to boost enlisted morale.
Photo courtesy of Robert C. Hanger

LSTs off Leyte — October 1944
The Battle of Leyte Gulf saw the first use of Kamikaze suicide planes.
Photo courtesy of Cliff Jones

Dr. Maxwell Berry and
Dr. Albert Sidney Johnson
New Guinea

General Douglas MacArthur
inspected their latrine —
a "ten-holer."

Dr. Maxwell Berry
117th Station Hospital, Leyte
Acting Commanding Officer and tropical disease expert
Photo courtesy of Maxwell Berry, M.D.

Buchanwald victims await
cremation, a ghastly sight for
the medical team from the
39th Evacuation Hospital.
*Photo courtesty of
David Robinson, M.D.*

Fred Olander's B-17 after third mission, September 12, 1944
Bombing of oil refineries, Brux, Czechoslovakia
Photo courtesy Fred H. Olander Jr.

Olander's fellow crew members, Tom Dugger and Gene Beaudoin, celebrate
completion of final mission before Stateside rotation
Photo courtesy Fred H. Olander Jr.

Fred Olander was shot down on his 28th mission, over Leipzig, Germany:

"We bailed out at about 5,000 feet and all were captured. Leaving the plane was one of the noisiest times, with motors roaring and wind swishing. But as soon as the parachute opened, I experienced the quietest time … there was no sound. The verbal parachute training we had slept through so many times came to reality and worked."

Lt. Fred H. Olander Jr.
Photo courtesy Fred H. Olander Jr.

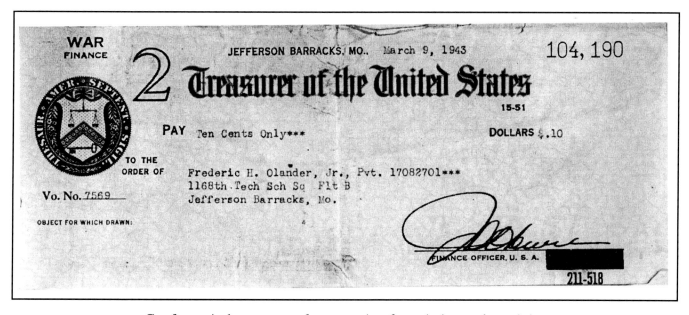

Car fare reimbursement after reporting for aviation cadet training
Photo courtesy Fred H. Olander Jr.

James M. Kemper Jr.
Photo courtesy of James M. Kemper Jr.

David Woods Kemper
Photo courtesy of James M. Kemper Jr.

1st Lt. James Kemper (left) firing 8th Cavalry anti-tank gun
at Japanese position, Luzon, Philippines
Photo courtesy of James M. Kemper Jr.

"The psychology of war is a queer thing. Your mind tells you that it is a sucker's game to go to the front — wars are silly, and dead heroes are dead for a long time — but other people go; it *is* an acid test and you wonder if you can pass it. You read about the Commando Kelly boys, and … first thing you know you want to go. A funny business."
— *David Kemper to his brother Jim — June 1944. David Kemper was killed in action in Italy's Po Valley two weeks before VE Day.*

Decorated U-boat officer
surrenders to British

On VE Day, German U-boats were instructed to surface
and report their positions. Two of them surfaced west
of the Straits of Gibraltar where the MacKenzie was
patrolling. The MacKenzie escorted its former quarry
to Gibraltar where the British accepted their surrender.

All photos courtesy of Albert C. Bean Jr.

U-boat surfaced and surrendered to American destroyer
crew.

U-boat crew surrenders
to British

"Merry Christmas from the Hatfields of Zamboanga"
Photo courtesy of Grant Hatfield, DDS

Grant Hatfield and pet monkey
Photo courtesy of Grant Hatfield, DDS

Anzio Beach smoke screen being laid down by destroyer and photographed from USS MacKenzie.
Photo courtesy of Albert C. Bean Jr.

Faded inscription reads: "To Ensign E.T. Matheny, USNR
With best wishes and many thanks for your valuable and efficient services on my staff.
C.W. Nimitz 1 Aug. 1945" — Nimitz was as respected and revered as any senior officer in the World War II.

Faded inscription reads:
"To: Ensign Edward T. Matheny, Jr.
with best wishes and with appreciation for his services on
Admiral Nimitz' staff.
C.H. McMorris, Vice Admiral USN
Chief of Staff Pacific Fleet and Pacific Ocean Area"

LST 572 (below) saw service in both the European Theater of Operations and the Pacific. It delivered troops and equipment at Omaha Beach, Okinawa and other battle sites.

LST 572 — Omaha Beach, France

Photo courtesy of Earl R. Stark

Author (left) with Lt. Don Chaney, of Fairport Harbor, Ohio
Fifth Fleet — Guam

Fifth Fleet Bachelor Officers' Quarters — Guam

The Philippine capital
was devastated.

The ruins of Manila
Only Warsaw sustained greater
damage among the martyred cities
of World War II.

Drawing by Jack B. O'Hara

Shyness was a trait foreign to most of Manila's children. They accosted strangers without hesitation, peddled souvenirs aggressively and bummed handouts from Army messes. In their war-torn city, the assertive child had the best chance of survival.

Manila Bay

Philippine currency backed by the United States

Worthless Japanese occupation currency

Manila's economy was ravaged by inflation. Japanese occupation currency — pesos and centavos — was worthless, and U.S.-backed Philippine money was in short supply.

CHAPTER TWENTY-THREE

The Occupation Continues

THERE WERE OTHER TRIPS about the Honshu countryside. Some were aboard other crowded trains, where women came aboard carrying heavy burdens or with babies lashed to their backs. Seated Japanese men gazed unseeing at these uncomplaining women, most of whom remained stoically standing throughout their journey.

The lot of Japanese women was hard; they were often beasts of burden. I wrote my parents: "In proportion to their size the women carry the greatest loads I have ever seen ... sacks of sweet potatoes, bundles of wood, household goods, and of course children. They move patiently, resignedly along, with straps biting into their shoulders, never protesting or complaining."

Women walked a respectful few paces behind their husbands. In immediate post-war Japan, they were still regarded as inferiors whose duty was to serve the male-dominated family ... tyranny of the eldest male was the rule in Japanese households. But change was in the wind; the following April, women would vote for the first time and several were elected to the Diet.

Jeeps meant chocolate and chewing gum. An English-language conversation book was already in circulation, with phonetic translations, and frequently during our jeep rides we were greeted by groups of children shouting "Harro!" as we passed. Urged by their parents to win the friendship of the Americans, the kids themselves soon discovered the generosity of G.I. Joe with candy or gum. Little girls often hung on the outskirts, and turned their booty over to a brother or another male member of the crowd.

Bob Hanger's Marines had the same experience:

"The children were the great fraternizers. Our combination of free candy and the novelty of a different race brought them out in droves. Where the children went, mothers followed, and they, in turn, were followed by the older generations, men and women alike." *Who's gonna live?* supra, page 52.

We shopped in the isolated town of Atsugi; bargains were more likely to be found in such an out-of-the-way place, far from any American base. In contrast, Kita Kamakura was now accessible to all servicemen, quite different from the quiet community of only a few weeks earlier. Now, the local merchants asked outrageous prices for everything.

* * * * *

The selection of General Douglas MacArthur to direct the occupation forces as Supreme Commander Allied Powers (SCAP) was inspired. The emperor's August 15 surrender broadcast disillusioned Hirohito worshipers, and was followed by the Instrument of Surrender signed on September 2 subordinating the emperor to SCAP. The Japanese people, accustomed to an imperial presence at the head of their nation, promptly substituted MacArthur for Hirohito. The haughty general, with serene confidence in the wisdom of his decisions, seemed born to the purple. Even in khaki he looked the part of an emperor — more regal than Hirohito.

From General Headquarters (GHQ) in the Dai-Ichi building, wholesale changes would be introduced in the structure of Japan's government, including a new constitution transferring ruling power from the emperor to the Japanese people. However, although postwar Japan allowed much more freedom than imperial Japan, for many Japanese GHQ stood for "Go Home Quickly."

Post-war malaise affected the American forces in Japan. They were combat outfits, unprepared for occupation duties. So long as the war endured, they were willing to endure — but their commitment was "for the duration." Once the war was over they too wanted the occupation forces to "go home quickly."

The destroyer Wren was anchored in Tokyo Bay:

"The novelty of Japanese liberties soon wore thin for the Wren's crew, morale was low and most of us hardly ever went ashore — we just wanted to go home." *The Sacrificial Lambs,* supra, p.246.

Letters expressed impatience. Scuttlebutt abounded concerning our date of departure from Japan. Meanwhile, aboard the New Jersey, mustaches were cultivated on upper lips — hairy surprises for wives and girl friends.

Everyone was now counting the days until return to civilian life. Discharge from the Navy was based on "demobilization factors." The formula took into account age, time on active duty, number of months outside the continental United States, and dependents ("dependency status"). A wife was worth ten points — a reason to cherish her not anticipated when the wedding vows were exchanged. The points required for discharge were steadily reduced, but my own return to civilian life would take many more months.

Even if the necessary points were accumulated, transportation was a problem. Pressure for repatriation (a process dubbed "Operation Magic Carpet") mounted at home, where the slogan "No boats no votes" attracted politicians' attention.

The St.Louis was part of the Magic Carpet fleet. Once back home and out of the Marine Corps, Neil Lombardi returned to Yale for his undergraduate degree, then law school at the University of Michigan, followed by a distinguished legal career.

On board the New Jersey, we received coveted samurai swords. Mine was protected by a scarred black scabbard that had been knocked about considerably — but its razor-sharp steel blade was in perfect condition. It had undoubtedly been a family treasure. The provenance of each sword was supposed to be concealed somewhere in its hilt, but I was never able to unlock the secret of my trophy.

* * * * *

Basketball games were played occasionally in a drafty old Yokosuka warehouse. I contracted a streptococcus infection from a floorburn in one of those warehouse games. Fortunately the infection responded to liberal doses of penicillin, a miracle drug that only recently had come into general medical use.

The polluted water of Tokyo Bay was also a source of disease. It blew aboard the New Jersey as spray, and dysentery was prevalent on the ship. I spent time in sick bay, with a high temperature and a very painful headache. Seriously ill personnel were transferred to a nearby hospital ship, and a few were even returned to the States. However the New Jersey boasted four doctors and a well-equipped dispensary, and it was the rare case that could not be successfully managed aboard the battleship.

I better understood the need for all of those shots back in Plattsburg.

* * * * *

On November 8, Admiral John H. Towers relieved Admiral Spruance as Commander Fifth Fleet. The new commander was piped on board and the ceremony of changing command was held on the New Jersey's afterdeck, in the long shadows of three sixteen-inch guns, photographed by a bevy of cameramen. Towers, one-time Chief of the Navy's Bureau of Aeronautics, had been an aggressive carrier admiral, an "airman's airman."

My service with Admiral Spruance was brief — only a few months. During that time I came into contact with him occasionally. He was a very disciplined man who valued exercise. He walked for two hours daily on his flagship's quarterdeck while at sea, and took long, contemplative hikes when ashore. He was considerate of his junior staff officers, and we respected and admired him.

The taciturn Spruance was the despair of the Navy's public relations staff, in contrast to the flamboyant Admiral Halsey. Indeed, the differences between Raymond A. Spruance and William F. Halsey were significant. Halsey, aptly nicknamed "Bull," sometimes found himself at large in the proverbial china shop. He was audacious in the early stages of the Pacific war, when Americans prized audacity more than prudence in their fighting men. A brash, rough-and-tumble fighter capable of an occasional blunder, Halsey professed hatred for the Japanese. He was "good copy" because of his colorful personality. On the other hand Spruance, mild-mannered and professorial, weighed every move carefully, minimizing risks before engaging the Japanese in battle. Whereas Halsey was indeed a "Bull," Spruance was aptly nicknamed "the Calculator." Each earned his own special place in the Navy's pantheon of immortals.

Raymond Spruance went on to become Cincpac, later President of the Naval War College, and, following retirement, Ambassador to the Philippines. In November 1973, Spruance received the ultimate accolade when the U.S.S. Spruance — the Navy's first turbine-powered destroyer — was launched.

* * * * *

Visitors in starched khakis and gold braid were an accustomed sight aboard the Fifth Fleet flagship. American admirals had their own barges and did not use the New Jersey's boats. However, on one trip ashore I was joined by a Japanese admiral. He was a small, ordinary-looking man in a drab, rumpled uniform. We rode together in awkward silence in the ship's Higgins boat, a floating cigar box built to carry a rifle platoon from ship to shore and held together by nuts and bolts manufactured in Kansas City's Sheffield Steel Works.

* * * * *

Western music invaded Japan long before the war. Now a Japanese swing band, complete with a hip female vocalist, performed in Yokosuka. One of her numbers was a heavily accented "Shoot the Meatballs to me, Dominick." (The word that emerged was "Meatbarrs" — the Japanese had trouble with the letter "l.") The group's efforts were discordant but enthusiastic, and appreciated by their audience — largely American servicemen.

CHAPTER TWENTY-FOUR

To Home and Back

KANSAS CITY WAS HALFWAY around the world, and going home on leave was only a fantasy until I met the air priorities officer for the Naval Air Transport Service (NATS) in Japan. Formerly with TWA, he had lived in Kansas City and we had friends in common. He could arrange air transportation … my own personal "Magic Carpet"! Class four priority was certified … minimal but sufficient to insure air travel as far as Pearl Harbor.

It was a white Christmas at home and the holidays with family and friends were joyous. I set a record for consumption of vanilla ice cream at the corner drug store. The family sedan was always available, as were pretty girls conjured up by my sister.

Time passed too swiftly. Some of my friends had already been released from the service; others had Stateside duty while awaiting discharge.

Clint Kanaga, now a major, was discharged from the Marine Corps shortly before Christmas. Later, he was appointed twice to Kansas City's Board of Police Commissioners by Missouri Governors and also served as chairman of the Area Transportation Authority in another gubernatorial appointment. Tom Thompson, home at last from the CBI Theater, made the acquaintance of his son born the previous April. Bill Deramus also came home from the CBI Theater to resume a railroad career that culminated in his election as Chairman of the Board and CEO of Kansas City Southern Industries.

Ace Bean returned to Kansas City in mid-December, after the Mackenzie was decommissioned. He became CEO of Tnemec Company, Inc., a Kansas City-based paint company doing business internationally. And Dave Robinson, now a captain, was discharged in December, 1945. He was awarded the Croix de Guerre at the direction of France's General Charles DeGaulle. He returned to Kansas City where he engaged in a distinguished plastic surgery practice and directed the burn center at the University of Kansas Medical Center.

The Woodsons, Bill and Allen, who had been rotated back to the States after almost two years in the Pacific and reassigned to new heavy cruisers, were both on shakedown cruises on V J Day. Instead of returning to war, they were discharged and returned to Kansas City.

By year-end, Art Doyle had accumulated enough discharge points to board a transport for home and return to law school in Boston. Later, he joined Bill Woodson in a Kansas City law firm, and ultimately accomplished much at the helm of the Kansas City Power & Light Company.

All of this was fair enough — they had an earlier start in the war. But I had to return to Japan, and on January 7, 1946, mindful of my low air priority and my deadline of January 15, I departed Kansas City.

* * * * *

Upon landing in San Francisco, I went immediately to the Oakland naval air priorities office to arrange transportation to Japan. I was shocked when offered a two-week ocean voyage to the Philippines and, once there, I would have to find my way to Tokyo Bay. Another air priorities station was located across the Bay in San Francisco and I rushed there, arriving just before the office closed for the day.

Inside, I met a lieutenant (j.g.) who listened politely, but confirmed that my prospects were none too bright in view of my low air priority. However, it was closing time, and he offered consolation in a neighborhood tavern. Here, our friendship flourished over bourbon old-fashioneds and, late in the evening, he suggested that a note to friends of his in the Honolulu NATS office would solve my transportation problem. Meanwhile, he persuaded me to enjoy the delights of San Francisco for another day. So the next evening, instead of winging my way westward as prudence dictated, I found myself dancing to the music of Wayne King ("the waltz King") at the Mark Hopkins Hotel — and I was now old enough to be admitted to the Top of the Mark.

* * * * *

The following night I flew to Honolulu where the morning sun colored Diamond Head as we landed. I guarded the NATS note in my pocket.

At the Honolulu air priorities office, the NATS old-boy network worked like a charm. I departed forty-eight hours later for Japan by way of Johnston, Wake and Marcus islands, scheduled to arrive at the ship on January 14 after again crossing the international date line.

Johnston Island, of importance solely because of its strategic location, was a small, flat fragment of land barely above sea level, whose only attractions apart from the air strip were the gooney birds. A species of albatross, these birds were graceful in flight, and absolutely hilarious with their lumbering take-offs and staggering landings on the sandy beach.

Wake Island was a tiny dot in the ocean … three linked coral atolls totaling less than three square miles. A naval air station and the most remote American island base, Wake was across the international date line from Hawaii, so the December 7 attack on Pearl Harbor and the December 8 bombing of Wake actually occurred the same day. It had surrendered to the Japanese on December 23, 1941 after a heroic defense, and the surviving defenders became POWs who would suffer the brutality of Japanese prison camps. American forces returned to the island on September 4, 1945. That day the Japanese garrison, bypassed by the Nimitz island-hopping strategy and decimated by starvation and bombing raids, lay down their arms.

We were on Wake only long enough to refuel and then departed for Marcus Island, 990 miles from Japan.

* * * * *

At Marcus Island, the NATS old-boy network failed me.

Flights from Marcus to Japan landed at Kiserazu airdrome, near Tokyo Bay at the southern end of Honshu. Because of recurring weather problems, aircraft departing Marcus for Kiserazu carried enough fuel to return non-stop to Marcus, a fact not adequately stressed within the NATS organization. Our plane arrived fully loaded and nine low-priority passengers were bumped to accommodate added petrol. I was one of the unhappy nine.

The authorities on Marcus Island now reluctantly entertained a backlog of thirty-four beached passengers, and the number was mounting with each incoming flight for Japan. My plane left without me, hauling fewer passengers but substantially more fuel on the final leg of the trip.

I would not meet the January 15 deadline ..."Absent Over Leave," or A.O.L. would describe my status. I sent a dispatch advising that I would require a #2 air priority to insure my timely arrival. There was no response.

Marcus Island was a dull, treeless place, barely rising above the surrounding Pacific. The Japanese garrison surrendered on August 31, 1945, turning over a coral island honeycombed by a network of underground defenses typical of the Japanese — interlocking caves, dugouts, and slit trenches.

Living conditions were spartan. We slept in tents devoid of screens, on cots without pillows or sheets. Lister bags stored lukewarm drinking water, reminiscent of Guam in the early days but without the Coconut Log oasis. Breakfast was an inflexible 0545 to 0630, even though many of us had no duties to perform for the rest of the day. Spam was a staple on every menu. But showers were available, and a movie was shown in the evening.

My A.O.L status hung over my head. Of particular concern was the scheduled replacement of the battleship New Jersey by the Iowa, as the Fifth Fleet flagship. I was to take charge of flag plot, succeeding the Fifth Fleet's senior plotting officer, Lieutenant Don Chaney. Chaney anticipated returning Stateside with the New Jersey and I did not look forward to our reunion if I failed to relieve him in time. So, I pestered the air transport office.

* * * * *

Finally, my persistence was rewarded. On January 17, the NATS agent on Marcus relented and added my name to the passenger manifest for that day's Honolulu-Japan flight.

The flying weather was as bad as advertised and the trip to Kiserazu required an uncomfortable six hours. Our unheated plane lacked seat belts, and we were buffeted in the hard bucket seats by a strong headwind tossing the aircraft up and down. And when we climbed out of the plane's hatch at Kisarazu we were hammered by a 50-mile per hour gale.

The next morning, I caught a Marine flight for the short hop over Tokyo Bay to the air field at Yokosuka. I was relieved to see the New Jersey still riding at anchor out in the Bay ... the Iowa had yet to arrive. Soon I was back on board, a couple of days late but no one seemed to mind.

CHAPTER TWENTY-FIVE

Navy Life

ON THE DAY AFTER MY RETURN, a further change of command occurred. Admiral Towers was succeeded by Vice Admiral Frederick C. Sherman, another carrier admiral. The Navy's change of command ceremony had altered little since John Paul Jones, and the transition was marked by considerable pomp and circumstance although the Fifth Fleet's size had dwindled significantly.

January 27, the Iowa dropped anchor in Yokosuka harbor. As a new battleship, the New Jersey's twin sister had carried President Roosevelt to Casablanca in November 1943 en route to the first Teheran conference. Beginning in early January, 1944, she had been in Pacific waters — like her sibling escorting carrier raids and supporting amphibious operations. As a part of the Third Fleet, she had followed the Missouri into Tokyo Bay for the surrender ceremony before returning Stateside.

The following day, we loaded everything on an LCT for transfer to the Iowa. LCTs, manufactured by the Darby company in Kansas City, were smaller versions of the LST ... slow and cumbersome, but workhorses. We shoved off for our new home, and were back in business by mid-afternoon.

We watched the New Jersey weigh anchor and serenely depart for the West Coast. We knew that she was propelled through the water by monster screws driven by giant turbines, but their labors were hidden from sight as she eased out of the harbor. We fervently hoped to be making the same voyage soon.

* * * * *

I was appointed to a personnel board to interview reserve officers, expected to apply for regular Navy commissions.

During the war, America's navy yards produced ships in large numbers, at great speed. For the most part, Navy reservists manned those ships ... thousands upon thousands of landlubbers, transformed en route to deep-water sailors and often sailing straight into battle at sea — a tremendous accomplishment. At the peak of World War II, reservists constituted more than eighty percent of the Navy's fighting force.

The captain of the USS Abercrombie, a DE like John Wells' Munro, recorded the saga of his ship in *Little Ship Big War,* 1984, Edward P. Stafford, Naval Institute Press, Annapolis, Maryland. The author quoted a Naval Academy graduate whose destroyer had operated with the Abercrombie off Okinawa:

> "You DE sailors did one hell of a job out there ... You went out there right out of civilian life, most of you right out of school or your parents' homes, with a minimum of hurried training, in little ships that could have been better armed and equipped, and you damned near did everything we did with bigger, faster ships and a hell of a lot more training — and you did it as well, sometimes better. " (p.317)

Now the peacetime Navy's ships needed crews, and a campaign was launched to retain the reservists who had performed so well.

The recruitment effort did not enjoy great success; our Board had few opportunities to recommend reserve officers for regular Navy commissions.

One deterrent was the necessary but undemocratic caste system inherited from the British Royal Navy. Officers enjoyed the privileges of their rank and issued the commands, but there was uneasiness among reservists … we were aware of our deficiencies and our dependence on knowledgeable enlisted men.

Upon graduation from midshipman school, I had been provided with mimeographed instructions for new ensigns which cautioned:

> "Never call an enlisted man by his first name. In the case of leading petty officers and other men who have demonstrated their value to the ship, it does no harm to call them by the nicknames by which the rest of the crew know them. You can easily shift to last names, as occasion demands, without making them feel they're in the doghouse."

The same system affected relationships between officer ranks. Senior officers on the Fifth Fleet staff did not stand on ceremony, but Cincpac seniors could be more starchy. Many years after the war, now a practicing lawyer, I wrote to congratulate one of my former Cincpac superiors (a Navy reservist) upon his appointment as an Assistant Secretary of the Navy. His response began: "Dear Matheny." !!

It was not uncommon on a large ship for a month to pass after reporting aboard before encountering the executive officer, the second-in-command and chief disciplinarian. It was my misfortune to meet the Iowa's exec almost immediately after our transfer from the New Jersey. Many peacetime customs had vanished with the bombing of Pearl Harbor, but the Iowa had now reverted to Navy formalities unfamiliar to me … as a ninety-day wonder, I had only known the easy practices of wartime. In the course of my first morning on the Iowa I was reprimanded by the executive officer (a "mustang," promoted from the ranks) for failure to salute, chewing gum, and assisting an enlisted man with a heavy box. Such pettiness underscored the tyranny of Navy life.

The Iowa's exec was probably irritated by the flag personnel now underfoot. The honor of hosting an admiral and his staff was lost on the ship's company. All of that gold braid — those "scrambled eggs" on uniform hats — demanded more attention to spit and polish, particularly in the peacetime Navy. The officers of the departed New Jersey were hospitable, happily fleecing me in their poker games and drafting me for their basketball team, but the New Jersey had been specially equipped to accommodate us. Its extensively altered flag plot, my work place, was pronounced by Admiral Halsey to be "the best in the fleet." The Iowa was not as well outfitted for staff use and retained a full wartime complement. So the presence of supernumeraries was an inconvenience.

It was at the evening meal that the Iowa's reversion to peacetime ritual was most obvious, with coats and ties required in the wardroom and band music accompanying dinner. One afternoon Earl Stark, whose bedraggled LST 572 was in the harbor, came aboard in his shirt sleeves for a visit. I invited him to dinner where, wearing a borrowed coat with shoulder boards promoting him two grades in rank, he questioned whether we served in the same navy. I was never able to lure him back to the Iowa. He preferred the informality of his LST.

LST 572 was decommissioned in Tokyo Bay, and afterward used by the Japanese to repatriate their countrymen returning to the home islands. Earl was ordered to the port city of Kobe and the LCI 41, where his assignment was harbor entrance control — alerting American ships to the location of mines still threatening harbor traffic. In the spring of 1946 he sailed the LCI to the West Coast. After his

Navy discharge, Earl Stark became an agent with the Federal Bureau of Investigation.

* * * * *

On a clear day, Mt. Fujiyama (Fuji-san) was plainly visible from the Iowa. The 12,390-foot conical summit of this extinct volcano, sacred to the Japanese, graced the landscape.

An eyesore near the Iowa in the harbor was the Japanese battleship Nagato, confiscated by the United States as war booty. The Nagato and her sister ship the Mutsu were the first Japanese battleships to be fitted with 16-inch guns. She was the flagship of the fleet that attacked Pearl Harbor, and later a part of the Japanese battleship force at Midway. In the battle for Leyte Gulf, the Nagato sank four smaller ships defending the American beachhead — an escort aircraft carrier and three destroyers. The Nagato was herself damaged twice in the course of the Leyte Gulf battle. Afterward she was transferred to Yokosuka where she sat out the remainder of the war. Now she was 38,000 tons of corroded metal, her superstructure marked by towers and pagodas in contrast to the uncluttered Iowa.

One day the Nagato was joined by another derelict, the Japanese cruiser Sakawa. She was small for a cruiser, not much larger than our 2200 ton destroyers.

Another storied war prize in the harbor was the German heavy cruiser Prinz Eugen, a huge ship the size of a World War I battleship but with sleeker lines. The Prinz Eugen had participated in sea raids with the German battleship Bismarck, later sunk in an epic battle by the British ships Hood and Prince of Wales. She had survived the war and somehow found her way from the Atlantic Ocean to Tokyo Bay.

All three ships were destined for Operation Crossroads, atomic bomb tests to determine the effect of nuclear weapons on capital ships. The condemned flotilla also included the Pennsylvania, once the proud flagship of the Pacific Fleet, and the Nevada. The Nevada, the target ship, was painted a brilliant red-orange.

* * * * *

The harbor at Yokosuka Ko took on a festive air at night. Red masthead lights hovered above the anchored ships. White gangway lights led down to the water. Yardarm blinkers winked. And searchlights on signal bridges intermittently unrolled bright ribbons of light across the harbor.

Noise carried clearly over the water. A program of popular music, broadcast by a destroyer's public address system, competed with the soundtrack of a movie on a nearby LST. And there was the rumble of a captain's gig returning a commanding officer to his command, the small boat's light bouncing and bobbing swiftly toward his ship's bright accommodation ladder.

A bugle played "Tattoo," and a voice warned all hands to "turn in, keep silence about the decks." The harbor became quiet except for the occasional homeward-bound small boat.

At dawn this was once more a Yokosuka Ko occupied by gray warships and serviced by drab small craft, tugs and trash lighters. The time-honored command: "sweepers man your brooms, clean sweepdown fore and aft" summoned crews to drudgery, followed by the grating sound of chisels laboriously chipping paint away from steel hulls ... the most hated job aboard ship. Salt water takes a brutal toll on a ship — eating away paint and rusting any surface left unprotected — and chipping and painting have been the bane of sailors since ships became metal.

* * * * *

The Iowa was the pride of the fleet in Yokosuka, but she was almost bankrupt of small boats. Debris floating in the harbor wreaked havoc.

Travel was especially hazardous at night — the water was a minefield of partially submerged logs and boxes and other flotsam and jetsam. It was the practice to reduce speed in order to avoid or lessen damage, but wrecked boats were still towed back to the ship.

Ensigns were assigned as boat officers for trips to the beach, but they were essentially passengers who knew much less about running the boat than the enlisted men comprising the crew. The coxwain handled the boat, and his skill determined whether or not his craft made the round trip unscathed.

* * * * *

The Iowa's officers hosted a party for the flag staff at the Yokosuka Naval Officers' Club, complete with 10 hams, 10 turkeys, and music provided by the Iowa's band. There were formal, printed invitations with a formidable list of honorees. The latter included sixteen senior officers in addition to Admiral Sherman, ranging from the chief of staff, Rear Admiral Wellborn, to the assistant flag secretary, as well as a Marine colonel and the British commander who served as liaison officer with the Royal Navy. I was among forty-two junior officers named. Admiral Sherman "received" from 4:30 to 5:00. Commanding officers from other ships in the harbor were also invited. The large party was paid for out of the treasury of the Iowa officers' mess. Since the staff junior officers owned shares in the mess, we helped defray the expense despite our honored status. Nevertheless it was a grand occasion. And because my mess bill was a bargain at $35.00 per month I had little cause for complaint.

* * * * *

A few days after the Iowa's party, the British destroyer Uranus reported that a volcano had broken the ocean's surface two hundred miles south of the entrance to Tokyo Bay. The following day, a reconnaissance plane reported the increasing size of a new island as rocks and debris were hurled several hundred feet into the air. This was how Japan was born, eons ago.

I joined two senior staff officers in the flag plane, to view the phenomenon. A gull-winged Corsair flew with us, taking motion pictures.

After almost two hours, we saw feathers of smoke on the horizon that became columns of steam emerging from a small rock formation, the new island.

The sea was rusty with ash for a mile around the site of the eruption. Rock and lava bubbled and churned, continually shifting, disrupted by occasional explosions, and pure white vapor rose several thousand feet into the air. The fragment that had emerged was the very tip of a great mountain that had begun to form in the ocean's depths long, long ago. It was a primeval sight, as we circled taking pictures before returning to Tokyo Bay.

CHAPTER TWENTY-SIX

Occupation Doldrums

THE JAPANESE PEOPLE were eager to cultivate the goodwill of the occupying forces. At first, Americans were not responsive to their overtures, remembering the atrocities of the Japanese military. But it was difficult to resist innocent children, and it was impressive that their parents remained respectful of tradition and custom while struggling for survival.

Putting food on the table was a constant struggle for a population already undernourished at the time of surrender. It seemed unlikely that Japan — exhausted by almost a decade of war, its cities leveled by massive bombing raids or scorched by incendiary attacks, its factories wrecked, and with few natural resources for rebuilding — could again be a major factor in world affairs. But the Japanese, over a span of fifty years, had converted an insular, feudal society into a modern global power. Perhaps the real wealth of a country lay in its people, and they could repeat the miracle.

The resilience of the Japanese people was now manifest on the beach at Yokosuka. The day of the surrender ceremony, women jammed roads leading out of Tokyo after a Japanese circular calling all Americans "beasts" who would attack every woman in September 2, 1945. But the Japanese had adjusted to occupying troops not the punitive barbarians they had dreaded. Unconditional surrender d cide. The streets of Yokosuka bustled with energetic Japanese, rebuilding

As Bob Hanger later wrote about his Marines:

"We were a strange bunch of conquerors, simply because we d that role. The typical conqueror loots, rapes and burns, and, had the r quite sure that the Japanese soldiers would have conducted themselves sic pattern. Their record was well established in the countries they sub the best of them.

"This is not meant to establish that the American fighting men a than Japanese. In battle, we were every bit as cold blooded, every bit a as cruel. But the violence did not carry over to civilians at war's end. J the United States occupation, and fraternization proceeded apace regar directives." *Who's gonna live?* supra, page 53.

I wrote home:

"The Japanese are now well-accustomed to their American 'mast eager to please they are not the timid, doubtful little people I remembe assured, confident that they will not be ground under the heel of their conqu

* * * * *

The occupying forces were far from home; connection with loved ones depended upon the mail. Mail call brought instant response and "sugar reports" had a profound impact upon morale. There was the occasional "Dear John" letter, unwelcome word that a true love had found another. But usually there were affectionate assurances that absence had only made hearts at home grow fonder.

Intervals without mail intensified the pain of homesickness for a young sailor from Kansas City:

"Tell Sam I made Gunner mate and I am going to get on a Destroyer … Mom, why don't anybody write beside you. It is really nice to get a letter from Everybody … Your Son, Virgil. P.S. Tell Glena Gene and Jeannette and Pat and Velma and Opal and all the rest to write."

Women wrote letters to strangers overseas so that they would have something from the postman. Censorship handicapped servicemen trying to write an interesting response.

Frank Cortelyou's *Log* contains constant references to mail. The daily letters from his wife — each one recorded by number and date upon receipt — were often received out of sequence, a frustration: " Wish the mail would catch up — this is just like seeing the last part of the movie when you first go in, and seeing the rest when you know how it will end."

For David Duncan, the mail was even more uncertain but no less important:

"Today was terrific. I got my mail. Ninety-four pieces all told. At last I know, dear family, what's been happening outside my little world." *Yankee Nomad*, supra, page 143.

The arrival of packages from home was always welcome and frequently surprising. I received Christmas and birthday gifts at intervals throughout the year. A few weeks after my Navy discharge, there was delivered to me in Kansas City a box of Russell Stover candy that had chased me all around the Pacific before returning to the city of its origin.

Mail runs might be interrupted by weather. The Douglas A. Munro was in Buckner Bay, Okinawa when a typhoon destroyed the fleet post office there:

"While in Buckner Bay, even though we were not ready to depart, we received a message to clear the port along with all ships because of an approaching typhoon … It was as if the whole ocean had been lifted into the air and was enveloping our ship. The waves were at least 100 feet high and we were steering a course that kept incoming waves on our quarter so that we wouldn't swamp. Standing on our bridge which was 40 feet above the water, I couldn't see a destroyer to our port only 500 yards away with a mast height of at least 120 feet … I learned later that this typhoon was one of the granddaddies of them all." John Wells.

Commanders realized the importance of those canvas bags stamped "U.S. Mail" and made every effort to insure prompt delivery.

* * * * *

One day I received a letter from Professor Warren Abner Seavey, of the Harvard Law School, informing me that I had been admitted to the law school and would be expected in the fall of 1946. I could look forward to a life after the Navy.

* * * * *

Scuttlebutt was chronic concerning our return to the West Coast. The China-based Seventh Fleet was to relieve the Fifth Fleet, but SCAP wanted a unified command operating out of Japan. The mounting influence of the opportunistic Russians was a concern — they had declared war on Japan just two days after the Hiroshima bombing, and following the Japanese surrender resumed a cold war against the West begun decades earlier. These considerations delayed our sailing for home.

* * * * *

Several of us paid a mid-March visit to the coastal town of Atami.

When an express train pulled into the Yokosuka station, we joined a mass of humanity in the crush of a third class compartment. I had not traveled by train for several months, and was more aware of the seedy clothing, the incomprehensible language, and the short stature of the people surrounding us. Above all, there was the relentless pressure of passengers accustomed to train travel with an elbow in their ribs. But our discomfort was short-lived. The express quickly whisked us to the town of Ofuna, where we transferred to the Atami train.

The Atami train had a military car, equipped with plush seats and wide windows. It was roomy, restricted to Allied military personnel. At stations along the way, people forced their way into the other cars. As they boarded, they looked impassively into our comfortable, half-empty compartment and pushed on. To the victors belonged the spoils.

Atami faced a large bay called Sagami-Wan, on a section of seacoast acclaimed as the Riviera of Japan, and in happier times a favorite destination of honeymooners. Soon after Japan's surrender, the battleship Colorado edged into this same bay with care ("Into Sagami-Wan we went, prepared for any treachery." *USS Colorado Cruise Book 1942-1946.)* Now, in the Atami station, red-uniformed railroad officials sought to please. They offered directions, telephoned a hotel for rooms, and then ordered a taxi for us. The taxi was a charcoal-burning relic, but surprised us with a very creditable performance.

The Miyaki Hotel was tucked away up a narrow driveway, identified by a small wooden sign. Its construction was insubstantial ... five stories of wood, paper and glass. The innkeeper had been watching for our arrival. He collected our overnight bags and led the way into the lobby. I remained behind to pay the ten-yen taxi fare.

After negotiating a rate of twenty-five yen (about $1.70) per room, we replaced our shoes with straw slippers and, shuffling along, climbed four flights of steep stairs. We prudently carried our tempting, sturdy shoes and overshoes with us.

We removed the whispering slippers before stepping onto the sleeping rooms' soft, cushioned floors. The mistress of the inn offered to light a fire in the charcoal burners that heated the rooms. We accepted, and then departed to explore Atami.

A sign at a building entrance advertised in English a dance band called "The Golden Pheasants." Intrigued, we climbed a flight of stairs to a ballroom but the Pheasants had flown the coop, replaced by a decrepit nickelodeon stocked with American swing music records. A lone American soldier danced with a Japanese partner, while a group of partners-for-hire looked on impassively. Dance tickets were going begging at twenty yen a roll.

The shops of Atami exhibited the same ordinary items as Yokosuka. However, one store, operated by a small man in a skull cap, sold silk coats and kimonos. He offered to exchange merchandise for American cigarettes or gum, and chocolate especially interested him, but we lacked the inventory to do business.

An outdoor marketplace displayed meager food supplies: peanuts, clams, fish, oranges, and what appeared to be dried apricots.

In the geisha district, we were curiosities in our Navy uniforms; previous Allied visitors to Atami had been Army personnel. The geishas in their silk kimonos and distinctive coiffures were not shy. The traditional Japanese geisha was trained to entertain men in a variety of refined ways — dancing gracefully, playing a musical instrument, engaging in witty conversation. However, these appeared to be sisters to Flaming Mamie back in Honolulu.

We declined giggling invitations and returned to the Miyaki. Here we sat Turkish fashion on the soft matting for a meal of K rations and other plain food that we had brought from the ship … a feast by Japanese standards.

The next morning, the hotel receptionist called a taxi and soon another charcoal burner came chugging up, to take us to the station.

There was no military car on the Ofuna train, and our accommodations were cramped and crowded.

At Ofuna we learned that there would be a 20-minute delay for our connecting train to Yokosuka. This was unexpected; the most admirable feature of the Japanese railway system was a punctilious adherence to train schedules. As we stood on the station platform, unintelligible Japanese words suddenly babbled over the public address system, followed by the loud music of a military march. The people surrounding us had been bitter enemies only a few months ago, and I felt uneasy. Then our Yokosuka train raced into the station. It included a military car crowded with Red Cross uniforms, and troopers wearing the horsehead insignia of the American 1st Cavalry Division. The doors of the military car opened, we hurried aboard, and they rattled shut. Outside on the platform the Japanese pushed and shoved their way into the remaining cars. After a warning toot on the whistle, the wheels began to roll under us, and we were on our way back to the naval base.

Author beside Okinawan tomb
used by Japanese as a pillbox

ALNAV from Navy Secretary Forrestal
received by John Wells
Communications Officer, USS Douglas A. Munro
Photo courtesy of John R. Wells

Form 315

U S. DE

Heading:

NR S 918   142301/194   PRIORITY

ALL HANDS OF THE UNIVED STA-TES NAVY MARINE CORPS AND COAST GUARD MAY
TAKE SATISFACTION IN THE CONCLUSSION OF THE WAR AGAINST JAPAN AND PRIDE

IN THE PART PLAYED BY THEM IN ACCOMPLISHING THAT RESULT X PARA X THE
DEMOBILIZATION OF THE ARMED FORCES OF THE UNITED STATES AND THE RETURN

TO CONDITIONS OF PEACE WILL CREATE PROBLEMS TAKING PATIENCE AND CONTROL
ALMOST AS GREA-T AS THE TENSIONS OF WAR X I ASK THAT THE DISCIPLINE WHICH

HAS SERVED SO WELL TO BRING THIS DEMOCRACY THROUGH HOURS OF GREAT CRISIS
BE MAINTAINED TO THE END SO THAT NOTHING SHALL MAR THE RECORD OF ACCOMP-

LISHMENTS AND GLORY THAT RIGHTFULLY BELONGS TO THE NAVY MARINE CORPS AND
COAST GUARD X

                              JAMES FORRESTAL

From:	S ECNAV		Date: 15 AUG 45	Originated by:	Released by:
Action To:	ALNAV/194		Deferred / Routine / Priority XXX	Radio / Visual / Mailgm.	Restricted / Confidential PL / Secret PL
Information To:				142301/194	

Unit Comdr	Unit Eng.	Unit Gun	Unit Comm	Capt	Exec	Gun	Eng.	1st Lt.	Sply	Terp	Comm	O.O.D.	Med	Comsy	CQM	Yeo	

"On September 9, 1945, the Japs surrendered their occupation of Korea. I led a four-plane formation of F4Us at low level over a mass of humanity that surrounded the Capitol Building in Seoul. While we circled, the Jap flag over the Capitol was lowered and the American flag was raised! It was a thrill and a half to witness."

— *Art Doyle*

Arthur J. Doyle in his F4U Corsair, USS Antietem, Guam
Photo courtesy of Arthur J. Doyle

USS Birmingham
*Photo courtesy of
Wallace M. Burger*

USS Elmore
*Photo courtesy of
Clinton W. Kanaga*

"I was up on a five-inch gun turret, back slightly from the deck … just below me a catwalk connected the captain's quarters with the lower deck, where the surrender documents waited … A moment later, to my astonishment, General MacArthur and Admiral Halsey walked out on the catwalk right beneath me. Commodore Fitzhugh Lee really fixed me up royally. I certainly wasn't the person closest to the surrender signing table. But I did have one of the greatest overall views of the momentous pageant taking place aboard that battleship."

Yankee Nomad, page 195
David Douglas Duncan

Admiral Nimitz signs surrender document aboard USS Missouri,
before General MacArthur, Admiral Halsey and Admiral Sherman
(EPNH)

USS New Jersey
in Tokyo Bay

Scout plane, with pilot on wing, rejoins battleship as landing craft stands by.

Both photos from
USS Colorado Cruise Book,
courtesy of
William H. Woodson

Sailors enjoy rickshaw ride
in Yokosuka

Kita Kamakura railway station
The trains still operated.

Electric train — Yokosuka
Spartan and crowded, but punctual

Fire-bombed Yokohama
American strategists in World War II believed that moderation in war was a betrayal of those asked to fight it. America backed its fighting men with all of the resources and weapons at its disposal … prepared to bomb the Japanese back to the stone age.

Mountain road to Miyanoshita
The higher we climbed, the more rugged and beautiful the scenery.

Fujiya Hotel — Japanese post card

We photographed two smiling, kimono-clad hotel employees, rewarding them
with occupation currency … a pack of American cigarettes worth thirty yen
(about $2.00) on the Yokosuka black market.

Great Buddha or Daibatsue
in Hase

Although most Japanese were Buddhists, the government-sponsored cult of state Shintoism was a powerful force in Japan. More shamanism than religion, it fostered the concepts of Japanese racial superiority and the sanctity of the Emperor. The creed reinforced the Japanese war effort and was abolished.

Ancient Shinto shrine at Lake Hakadote
Japanese postcard

House of Peers chamber with emperor's golden throne, occupied by Hirohito on occasions when he was to address the House.

Ancient moat protecting Imperial Palace

Emperor's unassuming palace — Tokyo
Colorado Cruise Book
Courtesy of
William H. Woodson

Naval personnel and Marine detachment await arrival of Admiral John H. Towers. Doomed Japanese battleship Nagato in the background.

The Nagato was the flagship of the fleet that attacked Pearl Harbor, and later was a part of the Japanese battleship force at Midway. It was destroyed by atom bomb tests, at Bikini Atoll.

Admiral Raymond A. Spruance presiding at change of command ceremony

Admiral Raymond A. Spruance (left) and his successor, Admiral Towers, prepare for change of command.

R. A. Spruance, Admiral, USN
Commander Fifth Fleet
"He had a wonderful reputation to live up to, and he did."

The sea was rusty with ash for a mile around the site of the eruption. Rock and lava bubbled and churned, continually shifting, disrupted by occasional explosions, and pure white vapor rose several thousand feet into the air. The fragment that had emerged was the very tip of a great mountain that had begun to form in the ocean's depths long, long ago. It was a primeval sight, as we circled taking pictures before returning to Tokyo Bay.

Coeds' letters boosted morale.
Wilborn & Associates, Photographers

Transfer of mail — a precious cargo
Photo courtesy of Cliff Jones

-1944-													
201	1/23	221	3/1	241	4/12	261	5/1	1		6/28	8/3	8/11	
202	1/23	222	2/29	242	4/12	262	5/1	2		7/3	8/5	8/14	
203	1/20	223	3/1			263	5/1	1-Hosp		7/6	8/7	8/14	
204	1/26	224	3/1	244	4/12	264	5/9	2- "		7/6	8/11	8/21	
205	2/1 - 1/26	225	3/1	245	4/7	265	6/6	3- "		7/7	8/11	8/21	
206	2/10	226	3/1	246	5/9			4- "		7/9	8/14	8/28	
207	2/10	(2) 227	3/13	247	4/12	267	6/6	5		7/13	8/17	8/28	
208	2/1	228	3/13	248	4/12	268	6/6	6		7/13	8/20	8/29	
209	2/1	229	3/13	249	4/19			7		7/14	8/26	9/1	
210	2/10	230	3/7	250	4/17	(2) 270	6/6	8		7/20	8/23	9/3	
211	2/10	231	3/13	251	4/19	271	6/6	9	7/12	7/19	8/28	9/3	
(2) 212	2/13 - 3/8	232	3/13	252	4/17	272	6/6		7/14	7/22	8/31	9/7	
213	2/13	233	3/17	253	4/19	273	6/18		7/18	7/24	9/7	9/9	
214	2/13	234	3/22	254	4/24	274	6/6		7/20	7/27			
215	3/1	235	3/22	255	4/24	275	6/7		7/23	8/2			
216	2/13	236	3/22	256	5/9				7/25	8/2			
217	2/13	237	3/22	257	4/24				7/7	8/4			
218	2/13	238	4/12	258	5/1				7/26	8/5			
219	2/13	239	4/2	259	5/9				7/28	8/5			

Frank Cortelyou logged all letters from home — number and date.

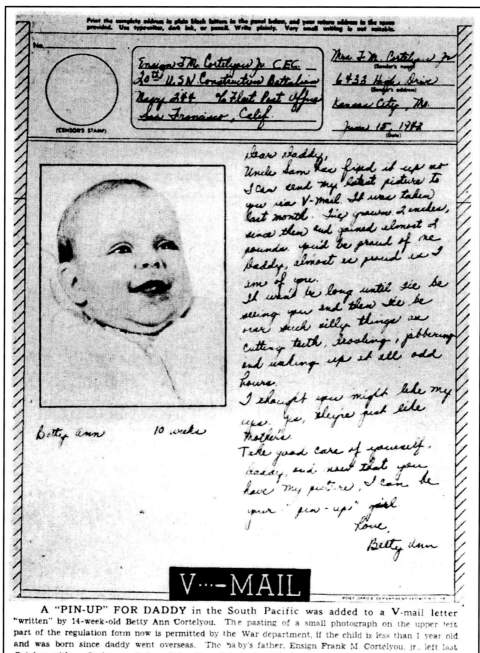

A "PIN-UP" FOR DADDY in the South Pacific was added to a V-mail letter "written" by 14-week-old Betty Ann Cortelyou. The pasting of a small photograph on the upper left part of the regulation form now is permitted by the War department, if the child is less than 1 year old and was born since daddy went overseas. The baby's father, Ensign Frank M Cortelyou, jr., left last October with a Seabees unit bound for New Caledonia. His daughter, whom he never has seen, was born January 25. She and her mother, the former Miss Betty Bean, are living with Betty Ann's grandparents, Mr. and Mrs. Albert C. Bean, 6433 High drive. Ensign Cortelyou, the son of Mr. and Mrs. Frank M. Cortelyou, sr., 421 West Sixty-first street, is a graduate of the engineering school at the University of Missouri, where he was president of Beta Theta Pi fraternity.

Frank Cortelyou meets his daughter.
Photo courtesy of Peter T. Cortelyou

The occupying forces were far from home; connection with loved ones depended upon the mail. Mail call brought instant response and had a profound impact upon morale … affectionate assurances that absence had only made hearts at home grow fonder.

Captain Gordon H. Robertson
Commanding Officer, USS Hornet (CV-12)
Photo courtesy of Gordon H. Robertson

Gordon Robertson, in addition to service as Commanding Officer of the Hornet on which he earlier served (CV-12), discharged multiple responsibilities including: Air Operations Officer on two carriers and Operations Officer on another, a year at the National War College, squadron duties including Commanding Officer of a Heavy Attack Squadron, temporary duty as Commander Air Force Pacific Fleet, and various staff positions with Bureau of Aeronautics, Supreme Headquarters Allied Powers in Europe, the Deputy Chief of Naval Operations (Air) and the Chairman of the Joint Chiefs of Staff.

Charles I. Campbell remained in the United States Marine Corps as a career officer, performing important duties at various locations including Fleet Marine Force Atlantic and Headquarters European Command. He returned to Camp Lejeune for his final tour of duty, retiring as a Lieutenant Colonel.

Lt. Col. Charles I. Campbell, USMC
Photo courtesy of Cathy Campbell

CHAPTER TWENTY-SEVEN

Sayonara; and Home at Last

AT LAST, the latter part of March we weighed anchor and departed Tokyo Bay for San Pedro, California. The Japan we left behind was dreary. Its seashores and mountains were beautiful, but its cities were devastated by war and its people everywhere were struggling to survive. We were glad to be going home.

During the war, sultry Tokyo Rose radio broadcasts described Japanese victories and sweethearts languishing at home. Although intended to undermine morale, the programs were popular with the armed forces and morale if anything was enhanced. Now the Tokyo Rose broadcasts were history, and our powerful flag plot radio picked up other programs from all over the Pacific. The closer we drew to California, the more West Coast broadcasts we could receive; American swing bands were particularly popular.

Over the horizon, home beckoned to the Iowa's impatient voyagers.

We crossed the path of a tidal wave born in the Aleutian Islands, but were unaware of the moment when our giant battleship rode over the mid-ocean undulation … just another swell on the surface of the vast Pacific.

For much of the voyage the weather was dismal, with bleak skies, strong gales, and heavy seas. In calmer weather, the gulls were frequent companions. They hung in the air above the ship and plunged in its wake for refuse. Their occupation was not very respectable, but their presence as we sailed an empty sea was comforting.

Almost daily, the Iowa conducted noisy firing practice with her five-inch cannon, and forty and twenty millimeter machine guns. Many servicemen suffered permanent hearing loss from gunfire. Occasionally the main batteries — the sixteen-inch goliaths — were discharged. Their deeper roars were not as deafening as the banging and chattering of the smaller caliber weapons but they shook the ship from bow to stern.

General quarters sounded one night, and fire shells from the five- inch batteries began to burst in the distance. They were highly effective, lighting the horizon with their glow.

Gunnery practice was expensive — the gunners were shooting up a lot of dollars. The exercise was important to maintain the gun crews' state of readiness, but the great ship's guns might never again be fired in anger.

* * * * *

When we dropped anchor in San Pedro Bay, the massive Iowa dwarfed the other ships. From the deck I could make out the fleet landing, and behind it in the distance rose the city of Long Beach, California. The promised land was in sight!

To reach Long Beach from the fleet landing of San Pedro, sailors crossed a narrow wooden bridge and followed a wide asphalt sidewalk. This promenade was called the Pike. On the seaward side of the Pike was a park-like plot of green grass with swings and teeter-totters, sand piles and tennis courts, and

105

beyond stretched the Pacific Ocean.

But it was the seductive district that had grown up on the landward side that gave the avenue its distinctive "Navy" character … strategically located to intercept sailors with several months' pay in their pockets and a compulsion to spend it.

During the day it was a frowzy place in the revealing sunlight, but night disguised the shabbiness. The invitations of concession-stand barkers filled the air, and bars and dance halls stood with doors ajar, nickelodeons blaring. A palmist's sign offered to disclose the future for a price. Tattoo parlors practiced their ancient artistry, and tailors altered uniforms and attached campaign ribbons.

The Pike offered an opportunity to blow off steam after long intervals at sea, but shore patrolmen twirling stout wooden clubs were also a part of the scene, curbing enthusiasm when necessary.

In contrast, the nearby Hilton Hotel's Sky Room towered high above the Pike, a world removed. Here the lights and music were more subdued, the conversation more polite. It held no appeal for the men of the fleet.

* * * * *

Dense fog often shrouded San Pedro Bay, challenging coxswains to find their ships. As they searched, they were careful not to pass through the outer breakwater and accidentally put out to sea. The Iowa's coxwain took bearings from various points in the harbor, as a precaution. He also listened for the Iowa's bell to punch a hole of sound in the fog blanket. The Iowa was BB 61, and at short intervals 6 claps on the bell would ring out, followed by a single stroke.

In mid-May, ComFifthFleet entertained the Brazilian Minister of Marine, like himself a vice admiral. But for the most part, the days of seeing VIP's come and go were behind us.

Perfunctory surveillance was maintained, from the Iowa's signal bridge, of a Russian merchant ship outside the harbor. She lacked diplomatic clearance and was denied entrance. The ship was a pawn in the rapidly deteriorating relations between wartime allies. Meanwhile, no small boats were permitted to leave the Russian ship for shore.

* * * * *

World War II had been fully supported on the home front. After it ended the public warmly greeted returning servicemen, celebrating with parades the victory in Europe and later the defeat of Japan in the Pacific.

I rode the Pacific Electric train from Long Beach to Los Angeles one day in the company of three Iowa officers. There we hitched a ride with an Army Air Corps captain in a big Lincoln convertible. A crowd had gathered on Hollywood Boulevard to watch celebrities arriving at a theater for a movie premier. As we drove past, someone shouted: "Here comes the Navy!" and so we passed by, doffing our white caps while everyone cheered. It was our victory parade!

* * * * *

The latter part of May the flag was transferred from the Iowa to the heavy cruiser Vicksburg. Flag plot personnel incinerated classified publications no longer needed, and in anticipation of my return to civilian life I relinquished my senior plotting officer's responsibilities.

The Iowa is now mothballed in San Francisco, a sleeping giant.

One morning, we moved down the coast to San Diego, passing the Russian merchantman still languishing beyond the outer breakwater.

In San Diego, the Vicksburg tied up at North Island. It would no longer be necessary to use a ship's boat — dry land lay alongside.

CHAPTER TWENTY-EIGHT

"Ruptured Duck"

ON JUNE 8, 1946, I received orders to proceed to the Navy separation center at Great Lakes, Illinois, outside Chicago. And on June 11, ComFifthFleet issued a three-word directive of immense significance: "Detached this date."

Air travel was out of the question — all commercial flights were filled. A mighty war machine was being dismantled pell-mell and the homeward rush was on. So I made the trip to Chicago by rail, sitting on my sea bag in the vestibule of a crowded Golden State Limited railroad coach. The accommodations were unlike the comfortable Santa Fe Chief compartment two years earlier, but I had been lucky to squeeze on board at all.

My notice of separation, dated August 12, 1946, summarized my Navy experience: enlisted 15 September 1942; entry into active service 6 March 1944; commissioned 27 June 1944; Plotting Officer, CincPac Staff, (Pearl Harbor and Guam); Assistant Operations Officer (Senior Plotting Officer) Staff ComFifthFleet (Guam, USS New Jersey, USS Iowa, USS Vicksburg). Net service: 3 years, 9 months, 29 days.

My great adventure was over, and a ruptured duck would be mine.

I received form letters from the Secretary of the Navy, James Forrestal, and from Harry S Truman, President of the United States, expressing the thanks of the nation for my military service.

The service that prompted those letters was expected. It never occurred to my generation that we had any choice except to answer our country's call to arms, in what was generally accepted as a just war.

Until Pearl Harbor, Americans resisted involvement in World War II except as "the arsenal of democracy" — supplying materiel to countries that were fighting our battles for us. It was hoped that war would not come to an America protected by two great oceans. But we discovered that the world of the mid-twentieth century was too small for isolationism, and made the painful, wartime progression to world leadership.

Pearl Harbor altered the life of every American, a cataclysmic event. During the long years between December 7, 1941 and September 2, 1945, the G.I. Generation endured considerable boredom, occasional terror, and the pain and death inflicted by combat upon young men in their prime. Some 1250 troops from Jackson County, Missouri died in action. The United States suffered 292,131 killed, 671,278 wounded, and a dollar cost of 288 billion.

Today, a younger generation can only wonder at the courage and sacrifice of those war years. In retrospect so do I.

I was extremely fortunate in my duty assignments. They were an interesting, sometimes exciting, continuation of my education. But many of those who fought that war paid dearly — for the future of all of us. Often fate intervened … not only as to duty assignments, but also as to where someone happened to be the moment when a shell or a kamikaze struck home.

"Combat is entirely a matter of luck and not being in the wrong place at the wrong time. It is also a place where you can discover the true worth of people and realize that it comes in all shapes and sizes." James M. Kemper Jr.

Those who paid the ultimate price were often the best and the brightest of our generation. The military took only the sound and among them death and injury often claimed the bravest, the cream of the G.I. Generation.

POSTSCRIPT

I WENT ON to the Harvard Law School, where the 1946 entering class was comprised largely of World War II veterans. Our clothing reflected our wartime service — uniform parts were much in evidence in the classroom and on the streets of Cambridge. Many had wives, some had children, and all had a no-nonsense if somewhat rusty approach to studies.

From the vantage point of well over a half-century later, it must be acknowledged that there were lasting benefits to veterans from World War II service — gained at considerable cost, for many.

One was the Servicemen's Readjustment Act or G.I. Bill of Rights, an educational bonus enacted by a grateful Congress and inspired by Topeka attorney Harry Colmery (Fred Olander Jr.'s father-in-law) — his proposal, drafted on a Washington hotel's stationery, was the basis for this noble legislation.

Another was the maturation of a generation, who grew up in a hurry and returned to civilian life with a sense of purpose. As Stephen E. Ambrose, author of *Citizen Soldiers,* once said:

> "Imagine flying a B-17 at 19, or being a lieutenant at 20 and commanding an LST that's as big as a ship. We don't give keys to the family car to people of that age."

There also resulted an unflappable attitude toward the inevitable problems of life — a perspective that has enabled veterans to distinguish setback from crisis, and to meet crisis with resolve and optimism.

Red Callaway gained special perceptions from his unusual wartime experience in race relations:

> "The soldiers of our company achieved personal victories as well. They were the last American soldiers to serve under the segregation policy that had divided the army since the Revolutionary War, and they not only endured this difficult period in American history, but performed well. Wherever these old soldiers are now, I hope they share with me pride in that long-ago war." *White Captain *** Black Troops,* supra, page 130.

In his Foreword to *The Greatest Generation*, Random House, Inc., New York, Tom Brokaw wrote:

> "At a time in their lives when their days and nights should have been filled with innocent adventure, love, and the lessons of the workaday world, they ... answered the call to save the world from the two most powerful and ruthless military machines ever assembled, instruments of conquest in the hands of fascist maniacs ... They came home to joyous and short-lived celebrations ... and gave the world new science, literature, art, industry, and economic strength unparalleled in the long curve of history. As they now reach the twilight of their adventurous and productive lives, they remain, for the most part, exceptionally modest. They have so many stories to tell, stories that in many cases they have never told before, because in a deep sense they didn't think that what they were doing was that special, because everyone else was doing it too."

Now it is important that their stories be told:

"As veterans of World War II 'take their liberty' of this world, what they have lived through and experienced in one of the most eventful times of our country — and of the world — will be lost to us forever unless it is set down and recorded ... We need to be about the business of capturing as much of their experience as possible in the short time left to do so." *DD 522: Diary of a Destroyer*, supra, from the Author's Preface.

"History is the part of the past that has escaped oblivion, and in order to escape oblivion someone must testify. Without Plato, Socrates, who never wrote a word down, might have fallen into oblivion. Without the Evangelists and the apostles, Jesus could just as well not have lived." *Come as You Are: Reflections of Everyday Life*, Peter Fleck (1933) Beacon Press..

ACKNOWLEDGMENTS

MEMORY CAN PLAY TRICKS. Fortunately, I did not have to rely upon mine. My mother saved my letters, and I wrote down my impressions of things at the time of occurrence.

I am grateful to all who supplied anecdotes, memories and treasured pictures for this book. These collaborators are far too numerous to mention, but hopefully the result is worthy of their valued contributions. Specific mention should be made of David Douglas Duncan who gave permission to reproduce and publish his historic picture of the surrender aboard the USS Missouri, and the picture of Mr. Duncan taken on Bouganville by President Richard M. Nixon, then a Navy lieutenant.

I am indebted to the authors of a few excellent World War II histories and biographies for refreshing my recollection of the big picture. The most helpful were: *Eagle Against the Sun — The American War Against Japan*, by Ronald H. Spector, published by Vintage Books, a Division of Random House, New York; *American Caesar — Douglas MacArthur 1880 — 1964*, by William Manchester, a Laurel Book published by the Dell Publishing division of Bantam Doubleday Dell Publishing Group, Inc., New York; *How They Won the War in the Pacific — Nimitz and His Admirals*, by Edwin P. Hoyt, published by Weybright and Talley, New York, *Embracing Defeat — Japan in the Wake of World War II*, by John W. Dower, published by W.W. Norton & Company, Inc., New York, and *Prisoners of the Japanese, POWs of World War II in the Pacific*, by Gavan Davis, published by William Morrow and Company, Inc., New York. Articles published in *The Kansas City Star* and *LIFE* magazine have also been of value. *White Captain *** Black Troops, Who's gonna die?, Little Ship Big War, Ordinary People, Extraordinary Lives, World War II — China Burma and India Theatre of Operations* (M.L. Thompson), *One Man's WW II, A Heritage of Excellence* — the history of the USS Hornet, the Journals of F.M. Corelyou Jr., Journal of Sally Kaney Tortellot Ruddy — *The War Years, The Liberation of the Philippines, Luzon, Mindanao, the Visayas, 1944-1945*, by Samuel Eliot Morison, published by Little, Brown and Company, *Ghost Soldiers*, by Hampton Sides, published by Doubleday, *The Sacrificial Lambs*, by William Sholin, published by Mountain View Books, the USS Colorado Cruise Book, *The Saga of the USS Birmingham, DD 522: Diary of a Destroyer*, by Ron Surels. published by Valley Graphics, Inc., *The American Beagle Squadron*, by Lawrence G. Burke and Robert C. Curtis and printed by the Lexington Press, *David Douglas Duncan: One Life, a Photographic Odyssey*, by the Harry Ransom Humanities Research Center, the University of Texas at Austin, *Yankee Nomad* by David Douglas Duncan, *My War* by Andy Rooney, published by Public Affairs, a member of the Perseus Books Group, *North American Aviation P-51 Mustang*, by Michael O'Leary, and *Over Here* produced by KCPT 19, most of them referred to above, provided specific insights. And for information about the war years in Kansas City, a thesis by Frederick Marcel Spletstoser entitled *A City at War: The Impact of the Second World War on Kansas City*, found in the Western Historical Manuscript Collection-Kansas City at UMKC, was particularly helpful. Also of great help in refreshing my recollections: the manual provided by the U.S. Naval Training School (Indoctrination) Camp MacDonough Plattsburg, New York.

Carol Leach of Edina, Minnesota provided expert counsel and editorial assistance in the early development of the manuscript; the late Captain Roland Petering, USNR, and Robert Bergstrom, Esq., supplied Cincpac anecdotes that I had forgotten or never knew; and many good friends and ex-servicemen encouraged me to persist in my efforts to publish the work.

ILLUSTRATIONS

Pictures from U.S.Naval Training School Manual are identified as USNT.

Pictures identified as EPH are from *How They Won the War in the Pacific*, by Edwin P. Hoyt.

Pictures not otherwise identified are from the author's collection.